Becoming Ethically Marketable

A Guide for Criminal Justice Majors and Recruits

June Werdlow Stansbury, Ph.D.

STAGGS
PUBLISHING

Becoming Ethically Marketable:

A Guide for Criminal Justice Majors and Recruits

June Werdlow Stansbury, Ph.D.

Published by:

 Staggs Publishing
P.O. Box 1565
Wildomar, CA 92595–1565 U.S.A.

http://www.staggspublishing.com

Cover illustration by Kyla Stanford (kstanford@houston.rr.com)

ISBN 0–9661970–8–9
Second Printing 2006
Printed in the United States of America

This book is dedicated to my God
and my beloved country,
the United States of America.

Special thanks to my "sounding
boards" and first reviewers:
Ridgley, my husband;
Readella, my sister;
and Gail, my friend.

About the Author

June W. Stansbury, a federal law enforcement executive and criminologist, received a Ph.D. in Criminal Justice and Criminology at the University of Maryland. She has conducted research in her expertise and specialization of "Narcotic Law Enforcement" leading to the preparation of papers, making presentations and policy change within her agency. Her doctoral dissertation, entitled "A Descriptive Exploratory Analysis of Corrupt Drug Agents and their Careers in Corruption" has formed the basis for several Ethics presentations and policy recommendations.

She has worked for a federal law enforcement agency for over 21 years. Over the course of her career, Ms. Stansbury has conducted successful investigations; been an academy instructor; a first and second level supervisor; and ultimately elevated to the ranks of executive law enforcement. Her geographic assignments have also been diverse including Detroit, Michigan; Baltimore, MD; Arlington, VA; Quantico, VA; New York, NY; and Houston, TX.

For over a decade, she has made hiring decisions about criminal justice recruits. Ms. Stansbury remains convinced that those interested in working in the field of criminal justice must behave ethically long before entering their chosen professions to receive serious consideration for employment.

Ms. Stansbury has previous law enforcement experience as a Police Officer with the Detroit Police Department and also with Central Michigan University's Department of Public Safety. Ms. Stansbury authored a chapter on Counseling Issues & Police Diversity appearing in Police Psychology into the 21st Century. She has been a speaker at the Academy of Criminal Justice Sciences' Conference, the International Symposium on the Future of Law Enforcement, the Interagency Committee on Federal Women in Law Enforcement Conference (ICWIFLE), Maryland's Annual State Conference on Teenage Pregnancy and Parenting, the D.AR.E. Officer's Training Conference and numerous other training seminars including on the management level. She continues to educate community groups in her areas of expertise.

Several honors have been bestowed upon Ms. Stansbury including performance awards for outstanding achievement, scholarships, a police citation, and being featured in news stories. Most recently (2004) in her capacity as a Senior Executive, she received a performance award from the Attorney General for Exceptional Service.

If you have comments for the author, she welcomes visits to her website at:

http://www.stansburysbeethical.com

Table of Contents

About the Author 4
Introduction 9

Part I — Practitioners in Criminal Justice

Chapter 1
Why Work in the Criminal Justice Field? 17

Chapter 2
What Can You Be? 21

Chapter 3
What Jobs? Opportunities in the
Criminal Justice System 25

Part II — Deciding on and Preparing for a Career in Criminal Justice

Chapter 4
"Know Thy Self" 35
Who are you? 38

Chapter 5
Temptations — The Field of Criminal Justice:
Is it too much for you? 43

Chapter 6
Integrity 51
Operating in the grey 53

Chapter 7
Can You Keep a Secret? 57

Chapter 8
Family, Friends and Others Close 61
Associations 61
Family 65

Chapter 9
Loyalty 73

Chapter 10
Truth and Honesty 79

Part III — The Selection Process

Chapter 11
What to Expect 93

Chapter 12
"Getting High: Not in the Job Description." 97
Chapter 13
The Background Investigation: Getting
to Know Who You Are 103
    Driving Record 105
    Money 108
    Criminal History 113
    Prior Work History 121
    References and Your Reputation 125
Chapter 14
Screenings 131
    Urinalysis Testing for the Presence of Drugs . 132
    The Polygraph Exam 140
    Psychological Exams 148
    Interviews 148
    The Dos 149

Part IV — You Got It! Keep It!

Chapter 15
Beyond the Hiring Process: Keeping it Together . 163
Chapter 16
Deciding to Do the Right Thing 165
Chapter 17
Rules, Rules, Rules 173
Chapter 18
Do Criminal Justice Professionals
have Freedom of Speech? 181
Chapter 19
Competency 185
Chapter 20
Abuse of Power 191
    Equality 192
    Unethical Behavior and the Code of Silence . 199
Chapter 21
A to Z for building a solid foundation
for your Criminal Justice Career 207
Chapter 22
Conclusion 211
References 215

Introduction

So you are all set. You have finished school and earned that four year degree; you have your best suit ready—in fact you may have purchased new clothes just so you look nice on your job interviews. Moreover, you are feeling very good about your accomplishments as you should—and now it comes time to go and seek employment in your field and everything will be well as long as you are able to jump through the big hoop of being ethically marketable.

Perhaps in other jobs you have obtained, it was simply fill out the application, go for an interview and then you got the job. However, positions in the field of criminal justice are not obtained with such ease. Due to a special level of trust your employer will require of you, there are more obstacles to be overcome. In determining if you are indeed qualified for a sensitive position, it is probable that an extensive background investigation will be required. Unfortunately, in my experience it is clear that many have not taken this very important aspect of the screening process into consideration as they prepare for their careers. It is essential that people consider and take steps to ensure that their character will withstand the scrutiny of a background investigation especially during a time when it appears that society is more tolerant of bad behavior.

I believe that the trend in this country is a lowering of values. Consider for example, a recent survey of Americans concerning their tax returns where 11 percent said it was okay to cheat "a little here and there," and 5% saying cheat "as much as possible" leaving just 76% to declare that they should not cheat at all (Anderson, 2003). But when you consider that in 1999, 87% agreed that cheating on taxes was unacceptable one can deduce a decline in values.

Even more startling and germane to our discussion is recent evidence of cheating by criminal justice students who had a unique opportunity to contribute in a meaningful way to the system many of them hope to enter. A poll was undertaken by California State University criminology students to help determine whether Scott Peterson, accused in the death of his wife and unborn child could receive a fair trial in certain counties. Subsequently, the judge ordered a change of venue with the poll's results playing a role in that decision. However, based on information provided by some of the students, it appears that some of the survey results were fabricated. The President of California State University issued a statement affirming an official inquiry into the matter citing scientific misconduct and academic dishonesty (Stapley, 2004).

Such an eroding of values causes a serious problem for law enforcement officials in the selection of persons for sensitive positions and can have negative consequences. The first is that this could lead to few people available to meet the standard for criminal justice positions; second, is that agencies may respond by lowering standards in order to be able to fill vacancies. In some instances, the latter has already happened. Consider that some agencies have gone from zero tolerance for past drug use to making concessions with drug experimentation for certain jobs. However, it has been consistently demonstrated that when standards are lowered to increase agency size great risks are taken concerning the personnel hired.

Law enforcement agencies present the most illustrative examples of what can happen when standards are lowered. In the 1980s the Miami Police Department lowered its standards and hired recruits unsuited to be police officers. The result was that by 1988, more than a third of those hired had been fired; and a notorious group of twelve came to be known as the "Miami River Cops" were convicted of serious crimes such as robbery, drug trafficking, and murder (Delattre, 1989). Commonly regarded as "rotten apples" by corruption researchers, I believe such persons should be screened–out and not work in the criminal justice field. However, I do not believe that everyone who has made mistakes in their lives are necessarily rotten apples.

The dilemma of every criminal justice administrator is that prediction of precisely who are the rotten apples is not exact. So if I am seeking to hire someone who has exercised poor judgment, irresponsibility, undependability or untrustworthiness, it is problematic in distinguishing between which persons have matured or changed to the point that these problems will not resurface and those who have not. The consequence of which is that many administrators will default to not taking the risk at all resulting in persons with questionable backgrounds not being seriously considered or hired. This posture could ultimately have an affect on your ability to obtain a position in the field of criminal justice especially if you do not protect your integrity and character.

Recognizing that more is expected of you than in traditional jobs, this book does not focus on those mundane aspects such as the mechanics of getting a job. Rather, it answers the question of "how" to make sure you *can* get the job. This is a "how–to" book in terms of suggestions and tips on passing through various screenings you will likely undergo during the criminal justice hiring process from what to expect before and after you get the job. I will focus on each of the important phases of the hiring process for the most sensitive[1] criminal justice positions but from the perspective of an employer seeking trustworthy candidates who have demonstrated a lifestyle of making the right decisions with uncompromising integrity.

I will present the perspective of a criminal justice professional based on 24 years of experience in the criminal justice field. All of those years have been in law enforcement providing me with a basis for presenting you with an overview of what I believe to be the most challenging of selection processes in the field of criminal justice. The good news is that if you are able to withstand the scrutiny of the kind of background investigation many law enforcement officers face, you should have no problem making it through the hiring system of many criminal justice agencies regardless of the position.

---

[1] This will ensure that all of the bases are covered. If you prepare for the most scrutiny, you should be able to pass any background check.

My service as a practitioner was with three different law enforcement agencies where I held a diversity of assignments including in executive management. These diverse positions presented unique opportunities for perspectives and expectations of ethical behavior from self, co–workers, bosses and staff I was responsible for supervising. I have learned much over the years but I assure you that still I am a long way from perfection. On the contrary, over time I have made regretful decisions. Writing this book has brought many of my poorer choices back to memory and literally caused me to cringe at times.

Most of the decisions I wish I could throw into the sea of forgetfulness occurred earlier in my career and were born of ignorance. I wish I had then, as you now do, a source of information that could be used to expose myself to knowledge that could have resulted in better decisions. I do not wish to come across as judgmental, but make no mistake there will be judgments made about decisions you make before and during your criminal justice career. Thankfully, as we mature, so usually do our decisions and thus our behavior. One thing I have learned over the years is assessing the appropriateness of sharing personal experiences. Thus, some experiences I will share with you and some I shall not. A primary goal I have is that while you read this you will inductively identify ways to deal with your own decisions as much as you acquire knowledge plainly. Discerning the appropriate situations for public disclosure in your life may be one of the most important lessons you learn over the course of your criminal justice career. When conducting the exercises included, think about which situations are appropriate for discussions with others and which ones should remain mental exercises.

I am very excited about this project. An incentive for obtaining a doctorate was the opportunity it would afford me to bridge the worlds of academia and practice. I have long believed, at least on the outside looking in that scholars often conduct research and write about stuff that rarely matters to the practitioner—the result of which is the practitioner's yawn accompanied by "so what" at research results. On the other hand, having practitioners engaging in research from the standpoint of scholars can be a scary thing in that the level of scientific rigor may be lacking. The yawn of the practitioner may be compared to a smirk from the scholar since a lack of academic standards result in no real basis for drawing firm conclusions or implications with confidence. Although this is not a research study—I remain pleased to pursue a project which gives me an opportunity to do just what I set out to do when I sought my doctorate in criminology—to do work that is useful to practitioners and hopefully regarded seriously by scholars.

I hope that one of two things be accomplished for prospective criminal justice professionals as they read this book: either your resolve is strengthened in choosing the right field based on your willingness and ability to continually build a character that will contribute positively to the field of criminal justice; or that you come to the realization that the ethical demands of this line of work are such that you have to seriously reconsider whether criminal justice (CRJ) is the major you wish to pursue. I see each of these extremes as worthwhile goals in that it is just as important to encourage and prepare those of you who selected the CRJ field for the right reasons and are capable of keeping your commitments as it is to help those who need more information before embarking on a career that could prove to be disastrous for them and their prospective employers.

Since your ability to enter a profession in criminal justice is dependant on your standard of conduct, it is important to know what is expected of you long *before* you actually seek employment in this field. It has saddened me to see unfortunate situations where people have planned to enter the field of CRJ, including obtaining the requisite degrees only to find that previous conduct impeded their ability to actually enter the profession. Becoming ethically marketable requires that you realize that it is just as important to prepare for this field with your lifestyle as it is to do so academically. To the extent to which one can assess ability to obtain work as a criminal justice professional based on past choices, this book will have accomplished a primary objective.

I employ a practical approach in a straightforward manner using current events to illustrate various points. To that end, Life Application Exercises (LAEs) have been developed and are included throughout this book to assist you with thinking about your stance on various subjects to help you determine the extent your beliefs line up with the standards of the field you hope to enter. Participation in these exercises should aid you in reinforcing values you already hold, and identifying those you hope to foster. Moreover, the results of some of the exercises may cause you to either sustain or question whether criminal justice is the profession for you.

It is essential that you are honest with yourself while navigating through these exercises to assess how you really feel. This will help to determine your "fit" to the ethical standards for criminal justice positions. If you feel that you are unable to be as honest as you like in a group setting, it is recommended that those exercises be done in isolation. You do not even have to write anything down, but you should come away from a given exercise knowing what your position is and how it will make working in the criminal justice field harder or easier for you. Finally, as so indicated, certain exercises are recommended during your meditation time due to subject sensitivity. Lets face it, you do not know if you can trust everyone to keep everything confidential.

A Chinese Proverb suggests that "a fool makes his own mistakes, but a wise man learns from the mistakes of others". Learn from the examples presented in this book that identify mistakes of others. Your willingness to do so can pay off by maximizing the likelihood that you will not unwittingly compromise your integrity and consequently get that great job in the field of criminal justice you are working so hard to obtain.

Part I

Practitioners
In
Criminal Justice

Chapter 1

Why Work in the Criminal Justice Field?

Have you ever wondered how people who have really great jobs got them? Perhaps you have witnessed interviews where others have spoken of sacrifices made to obtain the experience and education required to get the job. Maybe they even had to take jobs paying substantially less money to act as a stepping–stone to get there. However, what is less likely to have been included in these personal stories is what character requirements are necessary to *qualify* for the positions. Knowing the ethical requirements for hire in the field of criminal justice can help you better prepare for qualification.

Criminal justice is a wide field with law enforcement being just one of many careers. However, as with the high standards for hire, so also is the demanding ethical behavior expected of law enforcement officers which tends to be more narrowly defined in terms of what is unacceptable prior to hire and afterwards. This coupled with the fact that I am more aware of the requirements for policing, examples will be cited heavily from this profession. If you strive to maintain the ethical standards of law enforcement, you will likely have attained the standards of other criminal justice professions.

How hard it will be for you to maintain the ethical demands of a CRJ position will be related to your motivation for entering this field. For this reason, I recommend you take some time and think hard, examining yourself as to reasons why you have selected the field of criminal justice. You have probably already heard that, as a general rule, criminal justice does not present much legitimate work that you are going to become rich from. Criminal justice professionals, like everyone else need to earn a living so that they can take care of their families and their own needs; however, public service does not usually present jobs that tend to be high income producing as compared to other lines of work.

People sometimes make decisions without considering information which, if considered would help us to make informed and thus superior decisions. In the area of career selection, this frequently is due to a lack of available resources. This book will answer many questions you have, and quite frankly many you never thought about concerning the field of criminal justice from an ethical standpoint. It should aid you in identifying and or developing your stance on a host of timely issues. For example, in the selection of a career you should consider your salary requirements. In other words, based on the standard of living you want for you and your family, you should assess how much money you will need to make.

In making such an assessment, you might automatically rule out criminal justice as a profession as salaries tend to be lower in public service occupations compared to positions in the private sector. And the time to research and determine this is not after you have started in a position. Consider for example, that some of the post–9/11 linguists, computer experts, financial trackers, and even agents accepting jobs with the Federal Bureau of Investigation quit after only a short time. Reasons cited to the American Police Beat (2003) surrounded low pay. Of course the agents' situation differs in that they changed occupations versus were just entering the field which meant their standard of living was already established before they took these jobs. I believe it is easier at the beginning of your career to make a commitment to lower paying jobs because your standard of living is in the process of being determined.

You should not count on having the time or the opportunity to supplement your public service income by engaging in outside employment. Often criminal justice professionals work well beyond the "9–5" schedule that has been touted in this country as the normal workday. That fact is part of the reason that some governmental agencies disallow or restrict their employees from engaging in other work. For example, the Department of Justice website lists among the standards of conduct for its employees a prohibition from engaging in outside activities, including employment that conflicts with their official duties.

I am not saying that you cannot make a comfortable salary in the field of CRJ.[2] I am simply saying that compared to other professional type positions, you are not likely to become wealthy. With that in mind, if money is a very important thing to you—if you have always wanted to earn a high salary, be rich or if money is a very essential part of your life and the future that you see yourself in, you may want to reconsider whether or not you still want to go into public service.[3]

If money is not the proper motivator for entering criminal justice, what is? Many with experience will say that they became public servants because they wanted to do something for society. But corny as it sounds, having a burning desire to want to serve others is a noble reason for going into public service. Since oftentimes you will find that the work is demanding and thankless, an altruistic reason for entering the profession may be the one thing that will continually motivate and drive you throughout your career. It should also provide an adequate foundation to reduce the possibility that the temptations many face will come your way since exploiting the system is not your reason for taking the job. Remember one corrupt choice is not only enough

---

[2] As a public servant of 24 years, I have made a good salary I believe at every point in time. In fact, in my current position I have to admit I make more money than I ever thought possible. Of course this may be due to the fact that I never thought about the limitations or liberties associated with my salary in the field of criminal justice.

[3] Or you might want to delay your work into public service until after you have earned that "fortune." I have witnessed occasions for example where lawyers work in the private sector, and then become prosecutors or politicians although I have seen more of the reverse situation (public to private sector).

to keep you from entering the profession but also can be used to remove you once you are practicing.

Chapter 2

What Can You Be?

Aspiring to be a criminal justice professional, you probably have made some preparations to this end. Perhaps as
you selected a major you took some type of survey that helps
one identify which personal characteristics and traits
match up with a given field and or position. At some point
you became comfortable about the decision that you have
made. While not attempting to sway or change you from
that decision, a reality check can assist you in determining
whether you are likely to be able to obtain employment in
the field of criminal justice. There are many things in this
world that we may all like to do but everyone is not fortunate enough to be able to do all the things we want to.

There are all sorts of limitations, such as physical, intellectual, and economic, that can restrict a person's ability. In
the field of criminal justice there exists an additional limitation which may not affect our abilities but instead
opportunities—namely our pasts. Things that we have
done in our past, may affect our future. This book will aid
you in a kind of "back to the future" way by ensuring that
you are aware of the things you need to do (or not do) now
while in school to meet those expectations and requirements for getting your career off the ground later.

I am frequently mindful of a phrase touted in criminal
justice theory that you will undoubtedly hear throughout
your own studies, namely—"the best predictor for future
behavior is past behavior". In a quest to determine the extent of the past–future link, much research has been conducted such as cohort studies focused on periods of time
from juvenile delinquency to adult criminal behavior. Com-
parisons are made, and conclusions are drawn, and sometimes predictions are made—with a consensus that one can
predict future behavior based on past behavior. This
maxim not only rings true for criminal justice, but also with

much social behavior—including ethics and work perfor-mance.

If you take a moment and think about people you know, you can frequently predict what they will do in a given situ-ation based on how well you are familiar with how they have behaved in similar cases. It is rare that many of us are truly surprised by the things that people do that we know very well. And so it is that prospective employers, whether or not they are familiar with social science theories, will un-doubtedly weigh heavily your past, including positive and negative behavior as they consider your future.

Life Application Exercise

Recognizing that it is accepted in our society that what you have done in the past predicts best what you are likely to do in the future, how well do you think you stack up? Based on what you know about yourself, do you believe that much of your past behav-ior suggests that you are a good risk or a bad risk for a CRJ agency? Do you believe that the examples you used to gauge your risk are good predictors for how you will behave in the future with a prospective em-ployer?

Based on things that you have done in the past, do you feel comfortable and confident that you would be a good candidate? How competitive do you believe you are with other candidates based on just this fac-tor alone? If the worst were known about you to an employer, would the selection committee still feel comfortable recommending your hire, especially if there were a lot of candidates and only a few jobs?

To a large extent, you are the best judge of your past–future nexus because you have all of the facts—even if this side of you is never found out. You may feel that you are a good person and even if you know that there are things you are not proud of, you may not think that you are a poor risk. However, remember that you are not going to be viewed from your own perspective, but through the eyes of skilled criminal justice personnel who are very concerned about ensuring that they hire appropriate people for the right job. So pay close attention to the "eyes" as they will be presented in future chapters, providing you with some sense of what to expect. Knowing what prospective employers will look at and how it may be viewed will present you with an opportunity of seeing yourself from another set of eyes. This in turn should help you in making sound decisions about your career. Thus, putting you in the position to predict whether or not criminal justice is a field where you are likely to be able to secure the position that you have always wanted.

This career decision can be compared to that syllabus you get in school. It is sort of like a contractual arrangement. When a professor informs you of what is expected of you, you in turn think about what you want in the way of a grade and how much effort you are willing and capable of putting into getting the best grade you hope to receive. And then you decide whether to remain registered in that class, or whether to drop it and move on to something else. Sometimes you are not certain in the beginning so you opt to give it a bit more time for clarity. A worthy goal to commit yourself to before completing this book is having a real sense of whether the ethical requirements of criminal justice are too restrictive or not.

Chapter 3

What Jobs?
Opportunities in the
Criminal Justice System

Let's talk about the system—this criminal justice system that presents so many opportunities for work for those of us who decided to become public servants. Even though we would not have wanted it this way, those of us currently employed in the field of criminal justice, law enforcement in particular, as a result of the events occurring on September 11, 2001 now virtually have job security for a long time to come. Even with certain departments reorganizing resulting in lay–offs, there are many other agencies that have been more than appreciative for the opportunity to hire experienced help. This can be bad for agencies that experience a great exodus with their talent leaving for "greener pastures," but potentially good for you if you are searching. About the only thing that can get in the way of that job security for an experienced individual is ethical violations. This security is predicated on the fact that a past has not been sullied to the point that one's experience is over–shadowed by perception that you are a poor risk ethically.

A focus on offenders as they navigate through the system can be a useful way to identify various opportunities in the field of criminal justice. Well, it pretty much begins at the beginning—police are usually regarded as the first point of contact in the criminal justice system because their decisions form a basis in determining whether or not an offender will enter the criminal justice system. So it begins with the police at all levels of government from which they derive their authority including local, state, and federal.

With law enforcement agencies represented at so many levels, there is much in the way of opportunities for sworn personnel from police officer and sheriff deputies on the local level; troopers on the state level; and agents and deputy marshals on the federal level just to name a few. Moreover, in addition to sworn personnel, many law enforcement agencies employ other specialists such as forensic scientists, intelligence analysts, and other investigators also presenting opportunities in this field. It is estimated that there are at least 17,784 state and local law enforcement agencies employing a little over 1 million full time employees (Reaves, 2002). There are also several different federal agencies that specialize (i.e. the Drug Enforcement Administration, the Bureau of Alcohol, Tobacco, Firearms and Explosives, the U.S. Secret Service, etc); and depending upon which agency you work for determines the type of crimes you investigate and laws you enforce.

After individuals are arrested, usually their next contact in the criminal justice system is the courts. There is frequently a bail hearing to determine whether or not the offender is going to be released and if so what the conditions of the release will be. This step in the criminal justice process also presents career opportunities, such as, trial service case workers charged with making recommendations concerning release conditions (i.e. drug treatment). At all levels of government, there are court officers who are responsible for securing the court and ensuring that the offender remains in custody until released. For example, federally, the U.S. Marshal's Service has this responsibility while on the local level it is often the Sheriff's Office. Of course the professional positions of criminal lawyers on the defense and prosecution side as well as judges are usually also involved this early in the process.

Then there is the decision of whether or not a defendant will be released. If not released, the defendant will be remanded to the custody of an institution usually responsible for temporary lodging. At this point, the defendant has only been accused, and while there has been a ruling that there is enough to charge and hold the alleged offender since no conviction has occurred, it is usually off to jail—probably not a prison as such institutions are normally reserved for convicted offenders. Also this phase is regarded as an early stage in the process. So all of the positions related to temporary lodging, such as jail guards and criminal justice professionals responsible for prisoner processing, as well as housing individuals until such time that a decision is made about guilt are viable jobs.

In some jurisdictions, corrections and intermediate sanctions are contracted out; however, engaging in these positions is still working within the criminal justice system. Consequently, even these employees frequently are expected to under–go (almost if not completely) as rigorous of a background examination as those hired directly by state, local and federal governments. Thus, other than source of funding, there usually is little distinction between what work is actually done between those working within the criminal justice system that are paid directly by the government versus those working indirectly for a governmental entity but paid with funds through a contracting company.

If a judge so orders and the defendant is able and agrees to and meets certain conditions, he or she may be released pending trial. Some of these conditions may include remaining at home as supervised by electronic monitoring; or residing in a half–way house that may permit work–release periods. Each of these pre–trial conditions are now oftentimes handled by the private sector but ultimately responsible is the branch of government the offender is processed through.

Next are several legal proceedings where the defendant and the governing body are represented by lawyers. Prosecuting attorneys[4] are generally regarded as part of the

---

[4] While prosecuting attorneys are widely regarded as part of the criminal justice system, defense attorneys are not – a primary reason we will not focus on legal ethics. Lawyers have their own set of conduct codes which arguably may seem too lenient to some and more stringent to others. They tend to be more specific and much relates to bar regulations. I believe ethical standards for lawyers are less stringent than that of law enforcement staff because legal ethics appears more narrowly focused on the interests

criminal justice system. There are decisions as to whether there is enough evidence to hold offenders such as in a preliminary hearing or an indictment handed down by a grand jury. Having legally established the requisite element that there is enough evidence to demonstrate that a crime has been committed and probable cause to believe that the crime was committed by the defendant, he or she may be bounded over for trial.

The next stage rests with an important decision from the defendant as a plea is entered. And while there are an infinite amount of reasons why a suspect elects to plead guilty or insists on a trial, the decision is reached by the defendant, usually in consultation with a defense attorney. The prosecutor who represents the interests of "the people" are involved in the process to the extent that they may enter into plea bargaining with the defense to make a recommendation of a reduced sentence to the court in exchange for a plea of guilty to a certain charge. A judge ultimately decides on acceptance of a plea as well as the extent to which the prosecution's recommendation will influence a sentence. Judges and magistrates play an important role in the process and are also regarded as players in the criminal justice system.

If there is a trial, there may be many hearings where motions are filed and the defendant may or may not be found guilty. If not found guilty, the process stops; however, for our discussion we will next turn to a finding of guilt which presents the next stages of the criminal justice system. If an offender is convicted, either by pleading guilty or of a finding by a judge or jury, the next step is sentencing. The trial and sentencing process represents many opportunities for research of legal precedents and criminal history of the de-

---

of clients versus society at large. An interesting example of how these two professions are ethically juxtaposed was presented by FBI Special Agent Coleen Rowley (one of three Time magazine's persons of the year in 2002 known for her whistle-blowing of FBI's handling of information which may have predicted the terrorist acts occurring on September 11, 2001) at the University of Houston Law School, February 25, 2003.

fendant frequently conducted by paralegals and law clerks, positions also regarded as part of the criminal justice system. Depending upon a sentence of prison or some alternative, other institutions of the criminal justice system become involved.

A host of sanctions are available to the judiciary from probation to incarceration. Alternative sentences such as boot camp and drug treatment programs present various positions relating to offender rehabilitation. Sentences which include incarceration involve the correctional system which employs various positions including correctional officers. Even after release from prison though, certain offenders are monitored for a time by parole officers to help ensure that they remain crime–free.

As you see, the criminal justice system in the United States can be lengthy and complex depending upon how involved establishment of guilt or not–guilt will be derived. Having briefly examined this system it is easy to conclude it is comprised of many different segments focused on moving offenders along. There are aspects of the system that include handling offenders from their first encounter with police; through the various decisions made by offender and courts to establish release conditions and guilt; and beyond sentencing including incarceration, parole or even additional sanctions such as work release—all of which are included in the criminal justice system. Consequently, there are many different types of positions available in the criminal justice system to work in. And for the most part, these positions involve public service as various segments of the government are responsible for driving the criminal justice system. While there are some assignments[5] delegated to the private sector, such as electronic monitoring of offenders to assist governments, much is not.

---

[5] These contract positions can present opportunities for CRJ majors to pre–enter the field. Often contract employees are among those seeking permanent positions within various levels of government. It can be sort of an audition. If your performance is regarded as exceptional, it can increase your chances for hire.

Have you thought about where you will fit in? There are some important decisions you have to make in life and the sooner you make them, the better off you will be. One of those decisions involves what you want to do for a living. It is important to try and answer this question as soon as possible in your life as it will guide other decisions – for example which courses to take and what to major in as you attend college.

Life Application Exercise

The employment of correctional officers presents an interesting debate about the appropriate age one must attain for certain criminal justice positions. Belluck (2001) reported that a correctional institution desperate for prison guards had lowered the minimum age for correctional officers from 21 to 19. And while the lowering of the age is likely to increase the number of candidates, especially in positions not requiring a college degree — are 19–year–olds generally mature enough for this line of work? In the same article it was pointed out that guards could expect to have a demanding job, such as being verbally abused every day and having feces thrown at them.

Some would argue that work conditions such as these present a challenge for a person at any age, but how the problems are handled is the key. Is 19 a mature enough age to handle situations such as described? Having started my law enforcement career at age 19 (Detroit Police at the time hired starting at age 18). I believe that it *could* be. I think the determining factor is the individual and his/her life experiences. Albeit even at age 30, some will never be mature enough while others are mature enough even at age 18. A relevant question to ask yourself to determine if you are ready now, is how would you handle someone confronting or attacking you? Would it bother you or would you just see it as work? Would it be primarily your intent to subdue the prisoner or would you really want to get a good fight on? In your quest to subdue an offender – are you likely to want to use the force necessary to neutralize a situation or would you want to dole out some extra punches for your personal aggravation?

In conclusion, the criminal justice system in the United States involves the use of many types of professionals to manage the many phases involved. Consequently, there are many opportunities for criminal justice majors to obtain work. The biggest initial decision is for you to determine what you would like to do and identify a particular phase of the system in which you wish to work. Is it in policing, corrections, probation or parole or prosecution? Next, after assessing certain aspects of your personality, you can better decide if you would really like to work in the field of criminal justice. Part II identifies characteristics that will be useful to the criminal justice professional and his or her employer.

Deciding on and Preparing for a Career In Criminal Justice

Chapter 4

Know Thy Self

Deciding whether CRJ is the field for you may be quite involved. You must consider such things as how your life will change since it may be quite different from that of your current friends; and you must also consider what types of things you may need to give up to pursue this career. Some issues you should consider when deciding whether to pursue a career in the criminal justice field are broached in the following chapters. Can you keep a secret? Do you love money? Do you enjoy working long hours? How are you on self–control? Are you easily tempted? The common denominator of each of these subjects is knowing yourself.

This section provides you with examples of how you can live a life that can make your dream of becoming a criminal justice professional a reality. Unfortunately, since one can blow any chance of becoming a CRJ professional, we will explore dimensions that are destructive as well. No matter what point you are in school or your chronological age, you are creating a foundation for how you make decisions. And these decisions that you make will affect your behavior that can, and likely will be judged by you and others as right or wrong.

It is essential that you strive to make good decisions now that will lead to doing the "right thing," because it is harder to change behavior the further along you get in school and the older you get. Cheating presents a good illustrative example, because it appears to be a real problem in our society. According to the Josephson Institute, which examined the ethics of 12,000 high school students in 2002, 74% of student respondents admitted cheating on a test compared to the 61% who had acknowledged doing so in 1992 (Carlson, 2003).

In making decisions about studying and taking tests, you have to decide whether to study appropriately which will increase the likelihood of you passing tests or to cut corners and be tempted to cheat. When you make a good decision to study, there is less temptation to cheat on tests. But even if you do not study, of course you realize that cheating is wrong. And if you cheat on tests, I believe it will get easier to make the decision to take the easy way out of other situations and cheat. Not even considering the consequences for getting caught, how this erodes your integrity is immeasurable.

There are certain things you need to know now as a "pre" or criminal justice major to improve the likelihood that your character and integrity in consideration for a job will be judged in your favor. Anything that happens in your life involving law enforcement after age 18[6] is likely to be available to criminal justice agencies that may wish to check your background before hiring you. For example, did you know that having a drug conviction can affect your ability even to obtain financial aid for college? A recent law passed by Congress prohibits federal aid to college students with drug convictions. The law, which bans giving federal aid to college students with drug convictions was expected to result in the tripling of those turned down for this type of help (Levinson, 2001). But even if one does not depend on federal financial aid for college, having a drug conviction will adversely impact on job prospects in the field of criminal justice. This subject will be explored in more detail in Part III of this book.

How personal is your "personal business?" Do you believe that certain things that you do such as having heated and loud arguments or fights with family (which may be constructed by some to be considered domestic violence) or have a few alcoholic drinks and drive are your business and yours alone? The thing is that behaviors like this could result in your inability to get or keep a job in the field of criminal justice.

---

[6] And possibly even earlier than age 18 if it involves being charged with a serious crime, such as murder where prosecutors may charge one as an adult.

There are certain things that can be adverse to building a foundation for a CRJ career such as illegal activities. However, you should be aware that there are illegal behaviors that some would not regard as illegal that you may be held accountable for in your life in general but in the job hiring process in particular. For example, are you aware that it is illegal to know about the commission of a felony and to avoid reporting the information to the proper authority? This law is referred to as "misprision a felony"[7] and it carries a sentence of up to 3 years if it can be proved an individual knew about a felony offense, yet did not report accordingly. This statute has recently been enforced in drug cases to seize and forfeit the properties of landlords or business owners who knew drugs were being sold from these assets.

Avoid placing yourself in victimizing roles by persons who wish to minimize their risk of being detected as criminals. Drug traffickers and other predator criminals frequently front persons they believe police will not suspect to do their dirty work. Sometimes they do this and those used are unaware. You may wonder how this is possible, but consider for example that a means by which drugs are smuggled into the country is in clothing. Items soaked in liquid forms of illegal drugs make it easy for criminals to dupe the unsuspecting into becoming unwitting couriers. The thing is, aware or not, if you are the one "left holding the bag," you can still be arrested and prosecuted. The likelihood of something like this has become particularly poignant in light of a recent U.S. Supreme Court Ruling.

In Maryland v. Pringle,[8] according to Oyez (2003) the question presented to the court was this: If illegal material is found in a car and all passengers deny ownership, does the Fourth Amendment prohibition of unreasonable searches and seizures bar a police officer from arresting all the passengers? On December 15, 2003 the court held that

---

[7]Title 18, USC, Section 4.

[8]Maryland v. Pringle (No. 02–809) was argued on November 3, 2003 and decided on December 15, 2003.

the arrest of Pringle who had been a passenger in the front seat of the car while the cocaine was found in the backseat of the car was legal. The Court ruled that there was probable cause to believe Pringle committed the crime of possession of cocaine, either solely or jointly; and that the defendant's attempt to "characterize this as a guilt–by–association is unavailing". If you are arrested in this manner, getting a job in the field of criminal justice will not only be improbable, but it may be the last thing on your mind since you will be fighting for your freedom. More on this topic will be discussed in Part III on surviving the criminal justice hiring process.

Who are you?

Knowing who you are can be very helpful in determining whether a position in CRJ is right for you. In a friend's observation of what was perceived as rigidity in my personality, it was suggested that perhaps I should seek another line of work so I would "lighten up." My response to this was to make a statement which I have since repeated on many occasions: "I am not who I am as a result of what I do, but rather I have chosen to do what I do as a result of who I am". That statement, over time, has acted as a guide. In other words, I think it is important to select your career based on *who* rather than what you are. Even if the "what" you are qualifications are met (i.e. age, degree, health, etc.) knowing who you are may save you from trying to force a fit that may just not be you.

One of those "who am I" qualities that I possess that I believe has been helpful in my line of work include a tendency of seeing the world more in terms of black and white rather than shades of gray. While I do believe that everything is not necessarily defined in absolutes, many assumptions made in the field of law enforcement are. For example, law enforcement officers must frequently interpret acts as legal or illegal – felony or misdemeanor. When some incidents are viewed as misdemeanors, officers may exercise discretion as to whether an arrest will be made – but this discretion still does not take away from the fact that the act itself is regarded as illegal.

While there is a place for debate about whether an act should or should not be legal—the reality is that at a given point in time certain behaviors are regarded as illegal and a law enforcement officer engaged in an internal debate over the legality of a given offense may experience difficulties in discharging his/her duties—especially on discretionary calls. I believe an ability to view issues in black or white in many respects is based on buying into the concept of absolutes concerning right or wrong which can be helpful to criminal justice professionals.

Although it is true that each of us generally knows things about ourselves that no one else may, examining oneself can help identify what is held as valuable—in essence a value. This examination can focus on our likes or dislikes and comparatively can be used to determine what type of work is best aligned to these and other qualities. But one must go beyond even these interests to estimate whether you can meet the ethical demands of a CRJ position. It is important that you examine yourself and ask some of these questions before you obtain a job versus after being on a job for several years and then contemplate whether to start over.

Life Application Exercise #1

How do you view the world—in black or white or shades of gray? A controversial subject involves the use of marijuana, an illegal drug, for medicinal purposes.[9] Putting aside the separate issue of whether

---

[9]Even as I write this, the debate rages on. Moreover, a court battle is ongoing between opponents with the most recent December 16, 2003 Ninth Circuit Court of Appeals ruling in favor of two people who had possessed marijuana they claim was for medicinal purposes. This battle between the federal government and the State of California resulted in the decision that prosecuting medical marijuana users under the federal law is unconstitutional if the marijuana is not sold, transported across state lines or used for non–medicinal purposes (Associated Press, 2003).

this practice will ever become legal, currently do you think people should be arrested or prosecuted for using marijuana they claim alleviates a symptom of their ailments? Do you see the issue as right, wrong; more right or more wrong; or are you in the middle of the road? Do you think your position on this issue could affect your ability to make an arrest or press forward charges if you were a law enforcement officer or a prosecutor?

Life Application Exercise #2

Knowing yourself also involves things that you may have thought on, but never acted on. This subject can not be restricted to conduct only. What goes on in your mind, the things you ponder on are also important. For example, any dwelling on things that you know are wrong can be problematic. There may be some things that you have thought about to the point where you may have taken some overt steps in your mind. It goes from "gosh it would be nice to have $200,000" to thinking what you could do with $200,000 which turns into thinking about shady undertakings that you can get involved in to getting $200,000 (i.e. swindle or scheme). Sometimes what is thought about, while not illegal can certainly lead to taking it a step further in one's mind, actually seeing it from idea to reality can happen. Identify at least two things that you have been dwelling on. Are they positive or negative?

Life Application Exercise #3

I feel a need to once again remind you that I am not perfect, but I warned you at the beginning that I would sparingly point out my own short–comings. Learning from my mistakes and having a plan for the future has helped me tremendously. Over time I have developed a personal ethical vision for myself and I endeavor to use the following principles:

A) Doing what is right, is what matters most to me and beyond anything, it guides my decision making.

B) Getting wisdom first and then being in a position to impart wisdom is paramount.

C) Even when people "miss it", I choose not to confuse what they have done with who they are. It helps to keep focus that mistakes do happen and every mishap is not intentional. This perspective helps with aiding people in correcting behavior.

D) I *must* remain positive. Being negative is not an option.

Take some time to think about you. What are some of the things that have stuck with you and guide your decision–making and conduct?

Chapter 5

Temptations – the "Field" of Criminal Justice:

Is it too much for you?
Are you too much for it?

People struggle with temptations for all sorts of things. My biggest weakness is cheesecake. If it is set before me, there is virtually a 99.9 % chance that it will be eaten. To deal with this defect, I try to avoid having the cheesecake around me. Of course my biggest problem comes with the fancy sit–down dinners or high–end buffets where the cheesecake beckons me from the most attractive confection settings (although really the window–dressing is not even necessary to get to me).

I assure you that I have other weaknesses, but I use cheesecake as an example, because it clearly presents a situation where my will power is virtually useless. We all struggle with certain things that are more tempting than others. What we must do is identify how damaging the consequence of giving in to our temptations can be. It is particularly a good exercise to "soul–search" when we examine temptations on career choices. For example, in light of my "problem", it is agreed that working in a bakery is probably not a good idea. This chapter will discuss the serious temptations that many positions in the field of criminal justice present. If none of these situations are temptations for you – you are off to a great start. But if you identify any, then beware and take your concerns seriously, especially when you consider that acknowledgment from a point where there is no stimulus around like the cheesecake does not come close to having it set before you.

Most modern day corruption appears to be motivated by one of two failings—drugs or money. Of course there may be intervening variables such as catalysts that may influence the timing of corruption such as work dissatisfaction, disillusionment, family problems, financial trouble, and a host of other scenarios. But most everyone faces these kinds of situational problems at a given time and still manages to remain corruption free and I think there is an explanation for this.

I have this theory. On the subject of corruption temptation, I believe that people fall into one of three categories. First, there are people who will *almost always* engage in corrupt or illegal behavior because they are criminals[10] prior to their employment in the field of criminal justice and in some cases increasing their opportunity to offend may have even been their reason for seeking employment in the field.

The second type are people who *probably* will not engage in corrupt behavior, but might do it. They may or they may not. These, I think would engage in criminal corruption on a situational basis. Factors they take into consideration in their decision–making would include risk assessment – if they think they could do it and get away with it. Moreover, there may be some situational factor in that they may engage in some circumstances but they would not do it under other circumstances. For example, if they have a critical financial situation going, then that might be a factor. Perhaps, they are very dissatisfied at work and they justify their actions to help their situation and to get back at perceived enemies as work. In other words, if all the "planets line up" some people will engage in corruption.

The third type of people on the other extreme will probably *never* engage in corruption. You could put them into a

---

[10] These are those who may have engaged in criminal acts, but never caught. And as criminal justice majors, you may be familiar with the theories of deterrence. In the area of certainty of punishment, it is thought that as people engage in criminal behavior and they do not face "certain punishment" because they are not detected or arrested, they come to believe that they can engage in criminal behavior and not be caught.

room with a million dollars, they could have their kids needing expensive medicine/operations to live, they could have a horrendous boss and be as unhappy on the job as a person ever was, and they are still not going to stick their hand into the candy jar. It is just not going to happen.

As for what the distribution of this typology is among criminal justice professionals, I do not believe a bell curve is represented. But rather, the almost always corrupt and situational corrupt persons probably represent only a small minority. Nevertheless, the common denominator in many cases appear to be either the involvement of drugs or money as a motivator—and really the drugs–money nexus is so apparent that even when it is drugs, there is still an element concerning money—so we will start there.

I think that there are people who love money to such an extent that they would be willing to do anything to obtain it. I have come across a few people who fit this description during my career. They so intrigued me from the standpoint of being able to identify if they gave off any warning signs that I retroactively study them whenever their corruption[11] is exposed. I think about what things that the person may have done or said that should have alerted me to the fact maybe something was not right. And in my limited research into the behavior of these former colleagues, I have noted a common denominator among many of them in that they seem to love or need money more than the rest of us.

These people will "hold court" with you and tell you how to get over on the Internal Revenue Service. They frequently have a lot of investments and seem to spend a good bit of their working time on the telephone with brokers, and other business contacts. For any subject you are discussing with them, they frequently guide the discussion to money and the ways of making money—but in essence figuring a way to "beat" the system. Just earning a living is not enough; regular, sound investments are not enough; consequently, walking in the dark gray is embraced. As I look

---

[11] This seems to be especially true of those who were involved in theft of money, services, or other valuables.

back, on this diabolical few who frequently had stolen, these were the kinds of things that I heard them say. If you too find yourself where money seems to be much more important to you than the average person to the point where it preoccupies your life—especially to an extent that you are willing to do anything to get it and you have succumbed to temptation in the past, you may want to reconsider whether or not the criminal justice field is where you belong.

In law enforcement, there are many opportunities to see large sums of money directly because this is usually a criminal's first encounter in the criminal justice system—namely, where the arrest is made, where a search warrant is executed. Since law enforcement personnel engage in work that is closer temporally to the crime, the spoils of the crime are frequently on the scene; conversely, public servants for example who are at a different point in the CRJ system, such as in corrections, the same level of temptation on a daily basis may not be encountered although each CRJ position presents its own unique temptations.

You cannot regard yourself as immune from temptation of easy access to money if you select an aspect of the CRJ system besides law enforcement. There are other tempters in just about every aspect of public service. Public servants, especially those working in the criminal justice field, are sometimes solicited by outsiders to "look the other way"—to look the other way when an officer has pulled them over and they do not want to get a traffic ticket; for the correctional officer to look the other way as contraband is smuggled into the prison; for compliance personnel to look the other way when violations are detected; for the probation officer to look the other way and ignore a violation of parole. The field of criminal justice which employs hundreds of thousands of people is fertile ground for an individual who is susceptible to temptation in the form of corruption—so beware.

Misguided affections towards money can also motivate people to engage in illegal enterprises to obtain it. In the field of criminal justice this can prove disastrous in that there are many creative ways, while simultaneously appearing to be discharging their official duties, that corrupt persons can help outsiders. There are many examples of police officers accepting payments from criminals to provide protection to the illegal enterprise from the real "good guys". Those optioning this form of corruption use their identities as law enforcement to sneak through criminal activity. In short, the field of CRJ presents many opportunities by which one can make large sums of "dirty money" as a public servant. It would not be unusual for a drug trafficking organization to offer thousands of dollars to a border patrol agent to do nothing more than to permit a few seconds for them to drive through a border checkpoint without further screening permitting them to blend in with the hundreds or even thousands, depending on the port of entry, of legitimate crossing motorists.

No matter what the amount, if you can be bought at any price, you should avoid altogether this line of work. Are you a person who wants to "keep up with the Joneses"? Do you always feel that you need more and more? Is there never an end to it? We all strive to want to do better. But if you are a person who is very motivated by money, this should be a "red flag."

Closely linked to the weakness of money is that of drugs for two reasons. Drugs are a valuable commodity which can be liquidated and result in large profits—thus those who have stolen money on their jobs, often if presented with the opportunity because of the nature of their work also frequently have been found to have also stolen drugs. And nowadays, it is not unusual for law enforcement officers on all levels to encounter substantial amounts of drugs at one time, often street valued at tens of thousands of dollars. The other linkage to money concerns those who are addicted to drugs in that they engage in the reverse—addicts often steal money to purchase drugs. In both cases, regardless of motivation, drugs can be a strong temptation.

It seems reasonable to conclude that people who have utilized drugs in the past may have problems in the field of criminal justice, law enforcement in particular. The concern here of course is that most law enforcement positions present opportunities to interact with drug evidence in some manner. If you have used drugs before, especially drugs that are viewed as highly addictive which may be expensive or particularly hard to obtain; you at minimum have developed an appetite or craving for the drug and at worse an addition. Thus, putting one in a position of repeated exposure to that drug may create temptations where the wrong thing occurs. Instead of treating drug evidence encountered in CRJ settings in such a manner that it is submitted through requisite agency processes, one may instead confiscate those drugs for personal use.

You can appreciate and understand why criminal justice agencies must ensure that the individuals that they hire are not people who are likely to have a problem with drugs that may contradict their ability to carry out their work responsibilities, compromise investigations, and jeopardize the health and well being of the person and their co–workers. Perhaps it is a situation where someone did have a drug problem that they were able to deal with as a result of therapy and now they feel good that this will not present a problem in the future; however, if that person is subjected to drugs and the temptations, they may "fall off the wagon", and they may end up with problems. If you just think for a minute of the major problems that can be encountered from that person's own standpoint, such as destruction of the person's family; then you can understand that a CRJ agency has to be concerned with many things in this scenario including future lawsuits. The disasters with employees stealing drug evidence just run the gamut and are endless.

Life Application Exercise #1

Temptations are a part of life though everyone is not tempted by everything. Just because there is something set before you does not mean it is something you have to struggle to control. But there are all kinds of things out there that can be a struggle for you, as opposed to someone else. These are the things that you need to identify—anything that can present a potential weakness for you should be evaluated. Next, you should assess whether these weaknesses are something that could affect your ability to maintain your integrity in a CRJ position.

Life Application Exercise #2

A discussion in this chapter included a typology of corruption. Which category do you think you would fall into with respect to the three categories presented (almost always, maybe or never) of corruption risk? Again, in the criminal justice field, especially law enforcement, sums of money appear on the scene. And if you are someone who is predisposed because of past practices (i.e. stealing but never caught), you know what your situation is. You know if you have ever stolen money. You know if you have even stolen anything. You know if this is a character weakness for you. *You do not have to tell anyone.* But, you do know.

You may be telling yourself that you may have only done something inappropriate once or twice and each time was relatively trivial—what is the big deal? Do not minimize. A notion advanced in corruption study is that there is such a thing as a slippery slope (Barker, 1994) suggesting that people first engage in less serious offenses then advance to more serious offenses. And Gilmartin (1998) advanced the notion that corrupt officers first engage in acts of omission and then turn to commissions. Corrupt behavior may start off small as only a minor infraction in violation of the code of conduct for your particular job and escalate from there.

Seriously, if this is the situation, then you need to, for everyone's sake, avoid law enforcement and many positions in criminal justice. If you are someone who falls in the "might" category, where you do not believe you will steal money under most circumstances, but if you were in a pinch, and you did not think you could handle the pressure; or you have already been there where you have engaged in unethical behavior because your back was up against the wall, and you said look: "this is the only way out of a mess for me;" "I am going to have to do this;" "I am going to have to steal some money;" "I will have to swindle someone out of money"—if you have been faced with situations and have given into the temptation, do yourself a favor, find another major! Because you will likely bring shame upon all parties involved (you, your family, your co-workers and your employer).

Chapter 6

Integrity

What happens to be one of your most valuable assets? I submit to you that your integrity is certainly one of your most valuable assets. And it's very important that you do everything you can to protect yourself so that your integrity is never questioned. If you really want to enter your chosen profession, you need to take steps early on from the time that you first begin thinking about it to ensure that your integrity is not questioned; nor that you do anything to taint your integrity that may cause a prospective employer to conclude that you have judgment problems that may affect your decision–making in a negative way.

Perhaps the best way to measure integrity is to observe how one behaves when it is thought no one else is around or little opportunity of others ever finding out about a given act. Another factor involves the status of the observer. If the boss is looking as opposed to a co–worker it is natural for people to be on best behavior. In fact, a wise couple in their quest for identifying prospective leaders in their organization once assigned me to make some of these observations. That experience and every one I have had including my own supervisory insight has reinforced my belief that some people do things differently dependant upon who is watching but people of integrity do the right thing regardless of whether *anyone* is watching or not.[12]

I would go a step further than just observing actions to assess integrity because while an observer may be able to

---

[12] I am curious about how the new television series "The Family" airing on ABC will turn out. I believe it will be intriguing from an integrity standpoint in that unbeknownst to them, those judging the behaviors of the candidates will be the house servants—the "little people" often discounted by the arrogant in their treatment. In other words, no one will think anyone is watching when they really are.

make judgments about behavior, it is more difficult to assess what goes on in the mind or heart. In playing cards with one of my friends, if I take too long to decide which card to select, inevitably says "study long, study wrong". And she is usually right in that if I launch too far away from my initial or gut guiding thoughts, my decision usually proves inferior. Similarly, if you find yourself thinking about doing something that is not quite right at one time, what you may start to notice is that each successive time it takes longer to actually do the right thing.

Only you can be honest enough with yourself to determine whether you can be counted on to do the right thing in a career likely to present many opportunities to do the wrong thing without observation or detection and thus usually without consequence. There have been some though that have been found out and their situations provide clear examples of the problem with choosing to engage in a behavior believing it will not be observed. The use of business credit cards is one of them.

Many employers, including federal governmental agencies have attempted to streamline the procession of cash advances for travel by furnishing employees with credit cards which are only to be used for authorized official travel related expenses. However, many agencies with employees using official credit cards have experienced employee unauthorized use or fraud in varying degrees. Some of the ensuing scandals are included in the 2002 General Accounting Office (GAO) report that there was significant cheating on travel and purchase cards issued by the Pentagon (New York Times, 2002). The GAO's figures indicated that over 45,000 Defense Department (DoD) employees had defaulted on at least $62 million in official credit card expenses charged to the government – some 700 of these were military officers. Acknowledging that audit reports "point out instances involving fraud, misuse and abuse of [credit cards], the Under Secretary of Defense created a Task Force to propose recommendations to strengthen the credit card program" (Zakheim, 2002).

In the continuing scandal of government credit card abuses, one audit released in September, 2003 (Federal Employees Digest, 2003) found among the items purchased on the government's tab were a billiard table, costumes, caterers and a $2,900 aquarium. Credit cards also were used at a scuba shop and a bingo casino. Still other audits have shown credit cards were used by federal employees at brothels and sporting events. Could you, given a credit card with a substantial high dollar limit be counted on not to use the credit card for personal business, even if you had a personal emergency?

While misusing a credit card entrusted to you by a friend or family member may cause a strain on the relationship, consequences in a criminal justice position may be more far–reaching. For example, card misuse, fraud and abuse for DoD employees include termination of employment, imprisonment, probation, restitution, fines and demotion. Moreover, the DoD is even considering suspending employees' security clearances and possibly using state and local courts to prosecute violators (Kozaryn, 2002). If you think that you have a problem in this area, do you really want to subject yourself to a temptation that may result in firing, jail or probation?[13] While using official credit cards for personal use falls into wrong behavior, sometimes people engage in behavior that is less obvious.

Operating in the grey

Are you a "grey–hound"—someone who frequently appears to be straddling the line between what is right and wrong? Do you engage in shady behavior that is distasteful albeit legal? Lets face it, the whole point in majoring in CRJ is that you plan to work in the field of criminal justice. And if that is what you are going to do, then you need to take into consideration whether as a practitioner you will tend to op-

---

[13] The Defense Criminal Investigative Service has completed cases which has resulted in jail terms, probation and restitution fees (Kozaryn, 2002).

erate more in the shadows of grey or in black and white as much as possible.

The field of CRJ will present many opportunities for engaging in behavior that only you may question – it might be almost impossible for anyone else to know for sure. For example, at times you may engage in work, have to expend funds, and subsequently have to request reimbursement. Say it was a car wash on your work vehicle and no receipt is required. If you are inclined, you could "up" the actual amount and represent that you spent more than you really did. Some like to "stretch things."

A few years ago, I had lunch with a couple. They owned a business. During this lunch that I saw entirely as a social event, they briefly brought up their business. They explained that since they had brought up the business in our personal conversation that this justified them to classify it as a "business lunch." And because it was a "business lunch," they would be able to chalk up their portion of the lunch as a business expense for tax purposes. I feel that even if this technicality exists, referring to that as a business lunch was just pushing the envelope way too far. Or at least it was clear to me that this was something they should not have been doing. The ethics that govern business, at least for some may be substantially different from criminal justice ethics and if you think like those people, then criminal justice is probably not a good career selection for you.

Life Application Exercise #1

Based on your life experience up to this point you may not have been entrusted with the responsibility and authority to protect the government's reputation based on credit card usage. However, you likely *have* had opportunities to uphold or violate trusts placed in you by others. Think about the following questions and answer honestly. Your responses will help you determine whether your integrity is high or low and may identify weaknesses you choose to work on prior to your entering the field of criminal justice.

Has a friend or family member entrusted you with their credit card and instructed you to use it for a particular purpose, and without their permission, you used it for another purpose? Have you ever used your long distance or cellular phone substantially above the limit your parents or others set for you when they were paying the bills? Have you ever been instructed by your employer or parents not to make telephone calls to certain numbers with expensive services (i.e. 900 numbers)? Have you run up accounts such as internet or cable to the point your parents or other landlords had to enter into payment plans to continue service?

The aforementioned questions will help you identify times when you either upheld or violated a trust. For most, there are likely to be times when family members, friends or employers may express disappointment in your decision–making. What then? Do you get it together, stop, and do better? If you were confronted about any of these, or other behavior indicative of not maintaining boundaries or undisciplined behavior, did you cease? In other words, due to persistence, was the only way your guardians could get your behavior to cease based on *their* actions versus your own? Did certain blocking mechanisms have to be instituted on their part to eliminate the offensive behavior? If the answer to the last question is yes, you need to evaluate whether you are a person who can handle limits, as the field of criminal justice poses significant opportunities for you to get into serious trouble based on the trust that will be placed in you.

Life Application Exercise #2

An example was illustrated above showing apparent differences between ethics in different disciplines. This is an intriguing topic. Consider that administrators for different types of professions are likely to handle the same set of circumstances involving their employees very differently. For example, like what happens when one type employer detects drug use among its population vs. another. Medical doctors are encouraged to get help whereas, drug enforcement agents would be expected to resign or be fired from their positions for the same activity. It cannot be that the kind of work alone dictates an agency's position because most of us would agree that it is just as important for physicians to be sober as police officers. However, public service and the sub–culture of agencies are also factors. Select a criminal justice position you are interested in and a position outside of criminal justice and ponder on some scenarios. As a general rule, do you find that the CRJ professional is usually held to a higher standard?

Chapter 7

Can You Keep a Secret?

When people confide their innermost thoughts to you, do you find it hard to keep your promise of not telling anyone? It is important to explore the topic of keeping secrets because most employers require some degree of confidentiality from their criminal justice practitioners. While some of your work may eventually become public knowledge, much of it such as "tricks of the trade" or information you learn about subjects of investigation is never made public; meaning you may never disclose said information. It is not uncommon for a criminal justice employer to expect you to remain quiet about information you come to learn about during the course of your work.

In fact, some employers may even require you to make this promise as a condition of employment up front. Often this pledge will include a clause wherein you acknowledge the criminal or civil penalties associated with any unauthorized disclosures. Unfortunately, persons have been prosecuted as there have been too many situations in U.S. history where people have made disclosures of classified material to unauthorized persons.

It is true that "loose lips can sink ships." Sometimes things go bad in covert investigations with later discovery that the case was compromised when someone was talking "too much" to persons who did not "have a need to know." If the case was the only thing that suffered perhaps resulting in a failed prosecution that would be one thing, but the reality is that much worse can happen such as when the lives of undercover personnel are jeopardized if criminal justice practitioners talk too much.

Recognizing the need for confidentiality in carrying out the mission of your agency, the important thing to remember about talking too much is that in the field of criminal justice it can lead to murder. If, for example, a defendant learns the identity or whereabouts of undercover personnel or other potential witnesses, these persons could be assaulted or killed never having the knowledge that a threat ever existed. Not every breach of confidentiality has the same result, but they can always have serious consequences. For example, reputed spy and former FBI agent, Robert Hansen reported two double agents to his KGB handlers and both were subsequently executed (Havill, 2001).

Criminal justice professionals cause information to be entered into various computer databases about people concerning their criminal activities. Those working in the field of criminal justice also frequently have unlimited access to query these same systems that contain millions of situations concerning past activities as well as certain information relative to ongoing investigative activity. This presents many CRJ employees with opportunities to learn about sensitive information that may be a source of embarrassment to many – especially those having had limited contact with police and been able to keep that fact private.

Such persons may not regard themselves as criminals due to them having ceased the activity in question and or having had their records expunged. However, there have been instances where those working in the criminal justice system have illegally queried these data sources for their own purposes including for private gain. Those CRJ employees who make inquiry with motivations such as this subject themselves to criminal and civil liability as well as agency discipline. Some employees who have gotten into trouble in the past have done so in an effort to check out someone they are dating. However, if you think someone you are involved with merits a computer check – it probably is because you have concerns that you are unable to "put your finger on" and articulate, but these concerns are probably very real just the same.

A recent example of the use of databases for private gain involves a scandal in California. An officer there is being charged with tapping into internal computer files to track female movie stars, learn about any contacts they may have had with the police and then blackmailing them with public disclosure if they did not pay him (Singer, 2003). And one only need recognize how eager media sources were from the start to obtain facts on the allegations against basketball star, Kobe Bryant, to appreciate how valuable confidential information available to criminal justice professionals can be on the black market *before* the information becomes public. Criminal justice professionals must take care not only to avoid intentional disclosures but use caution to avoid unintentional ones as well that often results from gossip with friends or family.

Life Application Exercise #1

Do you tell things to others that you have decided beforehand not to reveal? Are most of these revelations to others about you or people who have confided secrets to you?

Every secret told to you should not be kept in that there are times due to legal requirements, professional ethics or just the right thing to do that you must reveal a confidence; however, this is probably rare. Have you ever made a disclosure that you do not believe you should have that resulted in serious adverse consequences for others?

Life Application Exercise #2

Not all secrets are created equal. Coincidentally, as this section was being edited I awakened to the knowledge that the President of the United States had made a secret trip to Iraq on Thanksgiving Day (2003) to greet and honor our troops serving there. It was reported that only approximately five people knew about this coup in its planning stages which spanned a few weeks. If you were one of the five, could you have been counted on to keep this important mission a secret?

Chapter 8

Family, Friends and Others Close

Do not be misled, bad company corrupts good character – NIV Bible, 1 Corinthians 15:33

Associations

Associations — they can make or break you. The things that people do when they are around you, especially bad things can affect your ability to obtain employment in the field of criminal justice. So be very careful about those you associate with. And once you get into the field of criminal justice you may find that it is not worth it to be around people who were previous associates. The reasons why agencies require their employees to minimize contact with criminals and what is recognized as the kind of aberrant behavior you need to avoid in friends or acquaintances is discussed in this chapter.

Lets say you are out with friends, and they are committing crimes and you do nothing about it. You may face some serious repercussions. Many criminal justice agencies have what they refer to as standards for your conduct that pertain to on–duty as well as off–duty conduct. One of these parameters is that you will not associate with criminals for obvious reasons. There is concern that criminals may draw you into their activities and it also looks bad for a CRJ agency if individuals who are viewed and seen as criminals are mixing with those who are charged with upholding the law. Thus, the sooner in life that you limit your associations with individuals who you can reasonably predict will create problems for you, the better off you are.

Another reason why agencies are concerned about hiring people whose associates are criminals is that it is something that may come back to haunt the organization later. In particular, these same associates could point an accusing finger at you later on and jeopardize ongoing investigations or cases that are about to be prosecuted. Moreover, a consideration on susceptibility to blackmail concerns individuals who may have undisclosed information about you that they can threaten to turn over to your supervisors in exchange for illegal favors. Thus the reasons are many why agencies prefer not to hire persons who have strong criminal associations. Moreover, even if not identified during the hiring process, this issue can surface as a serious problem later and still result in dismissal.

In general, a guiding factor to take into consideration when deciding whether to limit association with someone is whether a person frequently gets into trouble, especially with the law. Fighting, cheating, and stealing are regarded as bad behavior for a juvenile; but translated into criminal acts of assault, fraud and larceny or robbery for adults. It is also important to remember that once a person reaches the age of 18, he or she is regarded as an adult for purposes of criminal charging.[14] As a juvenile and before you get into the field of criminal justice it may just be an inconvenience to be around someone who engages in bad behavior, but many CRJ positions, such as that of a sworn law enforcement officer may require you to take action if criminal acts occur in your presence.

A scary thing about interacting with criminals is that not only may they engage in things that you are aware of, they frequently may be involved in things that you do not know that they are involved in that can result in you being drawn into their activities. Drug trafficking presents a perfect example of this point. Although illegal, drug trafficking is a business enterprise conducted in an underground manner resulting in a lot of things that drug dealers do to disguise their illegal behavior as legitimate. And since you are not aware of the things that they may do, you may unwit-

---

[14] And dependent upon how serious a given crime may be, some jurisdictions may opt to charge minors as adults.

tingly end up getting involved. For example, you may be out with a friend who tells you he is stopping to visit another friend when the reality of the situation is that he is actually dropping off drugs or picking up dirty money. Without you knowing what is going on you could unwittingly get involved. There have been situations where people of all walks of life, including students being detained, searched and even arrested under a scenario that they were in the company of friends dealing drugs at the time.

You may be asking yourself—Okay so maybe I just get detained. The police figured out that I was not really involved in anything illegal—what's the harm? I agree that police are usually pretty savvy on these things. They generally can put together who is culpable in a given situation[15] and distinguish between who is on the peripheral of a drug deal instead of direct involvement. However, if you are the only one holding the package, that is a completely different story and you are more likely to end up being prosecuted. Do not be naïve. Many drug traffickers are predators who will intentionally have acquaintances unknowingly temporarily store or deliver drugs to minimize their liability. Nevertheless, even if you are released, after brief detention, there usually is some record kept of your detention.

The question becomes, what effect, if anything can a detention have on your ability to secure future employment in the field of criminal justice? The answer would depend on the agency you seek employment with. Frequently such situations may only be contained in internal files since you were not arrested. But if it happens to be in the internal files of the same agency that you are seeking employment with, this could cast doubt on you. It may not be enough to eliminate your possibility of ever getting a job in the field of criminal justice, but based on the sensitivity level of positions you seek, you may be affected; the more sensitive the position, the more sources may be checked. Also consider

---

[15] Provided that the culprit is still on the scene. From time to time, persons are "left holding the bag" without even knowing it as the real drug dealer leaves the scene. Then the only person left, unless very convincing, is the only one available to "take the rap."

that even if an agency for which you seek employment has no knowledge or access to the internal databases of another agency, certain background questionnaires may require you to reveal these things even if there is no record of it. Thus, your best means of defense, is to avoid career damaging associations.

You also may be thinking "this isn't right." I just happened to be in the "wrong place at the wrong time." But going through life with that attitude, will not get you anywhere. Forewarned is forearmed. You need to understand that there can be consequences as a result of being in the wrong place at the wrong time. Because a lot of people are trying to get a limited number of jobs that means at each stage of the process is a screening mechanism whereby those who are hiring are seeking to "screen out" people so that they can reduce the pool of candidates down to a manageable number. And trust me; you do not really need that kind of headache. At times it is being with the wrong people at the wrong time, but being in the right place and choosing to do what may not seem as wrong at the time can also have adverse consequences on your job prospects.

Drug trafficking is an extreme example of what most of us regard as criminal behavior. But what about less obvious behaviors such as getting a good deal on goods sold in non–tradition outlets? You do not even have to be in the proverbial "wrong place" to be faced with having the opportunity to purchase "hot stuff." I have often times been in places, such as beauty shops where a parade of persons are permitted to solicit customers with virtually anything for sale. And it is very clear that these are not your typical vendors. Perhaps a few of them may have a vendor's license, but the types of items many try to sell, would raise suspicion by an astute person about the items' origin.

You need to consider if you are being sold something that was previously stolen. Will your purchasing a stolen item put you in a position where you could be charged with "receiving stolen goods?" Many people charged with receiving stolen goods have used the excuse that they did not know any better. But the law requires that we exercise good common sense (by the way, so will your employer) in our activities. So beware if you encounter associates who every time you see are trying to sell something that may have a questionable origin.

My own personal policy is to not purchase anything where I am suspicious about where it came from – whether it is at a flee market, a garage sale, or on the street. I avoid pawn shops altogether for several reasons, not the least of which I question the origins of some of the things sold. I choose not to deal in items which may be "hot" because in addition to facing the possibility of being charged with "receiving stolen goods," there is the issue that if you are not part of the solution, you are part of the problem. Therefore, people who steal regardless of their motives for doing so, if there were no incentive – a market with which to sale these items, then there is no real incentive to steal. In this sense, a person who purchases "hot items" is even more part of the problem than in some of the other examples presented. This behavior is to be discouraged especially for those embarking upon a career in the field of criminal justice.

You may be saying to yourself that you do not have friends like those described in this chapter. You may be right, but you do not want to find out the hard way that you are wrong. Your future is worth it for you to try and learn as much as you can about the character of your friends and not ignore warning signs that you may observe. You are likely learning in class about the various theories of criminal offending – include electives in your studies that identify the types of things various offenders do that would alert you early about criminal behavior so you can avoid these associates. It is harder to disassociate someone you may have come to like than it is to avoid them from the start.

Family

So what about your family? Can family have the same adverse effect on your CRJ career as do associates? It is true what they say in that "you can choose your friends but you can't choose your family." Family is an institution that you are born into. You have parents, sisters, brothers, aunts, uncles, cousins or other family members that may be involved in some criminal behavior or other negative stuff. You may have already been in situations where you have encountered certain family members whose behavior has made you uncomfortable. Although not personally involved in their activities, you have wondered if maybe a time would come when the police will swoop down on them and you possibly could get caught in the middle. Perhaps family members are involved in something potentially violent such as gang activity or drug dealing wherein you have worried their activities could put you in danger. What do you do when you have a family member that is involved in these kinds of things?

I once listened to a radio talk show where the participants had a discussion on this issue. The consensus was that if you have a family member involved in something as terrible as criminal offending that can create problems for you personally, the best thing to is to avoid or at best minimize contact with that individual so that you are not in harms way. As adverse consequences go beyond finding a good job, this is sound advice even if you are not seeking employment in the field of criminal justice. Notwithstanding, if you are not involved in their criminal offending, merely being related should not pose serious career problems.

No one is likely to turn you down for work solely because you have a family member involved in criminal behavior unless it is determined that you were also involved in the criminal offending. But the extent to which you spend time with this particular family member may become a subject of discussion in projecting what your level of contact might be with this individual if you are hired. For most agencies, this would not pertain to persons with a criminal history in the distant past, who were duly punished, and are no longer involved in criminal offending.

Active offending is another story though. The concern is whether your continual association with someone engaged in criminal behavior, even if it is a family member can adversely impact your career and tarnish the agency's reputation. An example of this kind of scenario involved a military officer who was assigned overseas in a South American country in charge of the United States counter-narcotics effort there. One day his wife was arrested for sending heroin from overseas into the United States (Feuer, 2000). What effect do you think this scandal had on a) her husband's career; b) on the military branch of government that he served; and c) on perception of the counter-narcotic effort to citizens of the U.S. and the South American country?

In fact, this incident brought embarrassment and shame to the husband and his employer as there was quite a bit of press coverage. What made this particular story more newsworthy was the drug importer's husband's high level position and each time there was a court action, the story again appeared in newspapers. By the way, reports indicated that the military officer was immediately reassigned from that post back to the U.S. So while it is easy to believe that because you yourself are not involved in bad behavior, still know that you can feel the ill effects of a family member's dark activities especially one residing in your household. There are even some employers that may withhold a security clearance if it is determined that you have someone living with you that is engaged in criminal behavior. Employers know how easy it is for you to get caught up in the madness.

Before you rush to judge your chosen profession harshly, understand that concern may also stem from the fact that criminals to whom you are very close may taint you. Interaction with family can shape who you are. While you personally may not be inclined to engage in criminal behavior, you may become overly sympathetic to those close to you to such an extent you become vulnerable to corruption. Say a family member with this baggage influences you to help them by using your CRJ position in some way. It has happened before.

One situation I am aware of involved an older man dealing drugs. I regard 50s as older for drug dealers because by that point in their life they are usually either dead or in jail—or in some very rare cases "retired" from the profession. But this guy had a daughter as well as a son–in–law who were both police officers. If known, this fact was apparently not held against the daughter because her father was a reputed dealer when she was hired as a police officer. Her husband, who was a sergeant, ended up working narcotics investigations at the same time his father–in–law was an active and significant drug trafficker. As time went on a breech occurred, although perhaps not immediately. Maybe the father was leaning on the daughter and the daughter in turn convinced her husband to divulge information. Ultimately, the son–in–law sergeant ended up compromising an investigation concerning the father. Someone could have gotten hurt as a result of this disclosure and that is why this kind of situation is so dangerous. Eventually, after the CRJ agency proved that the daughter and son–in–law had turned confidential information over to the father, they both were separated from the department. This is a very serious and sobering case in point. The lesson to take away from this situation is that if you have family members that you know are engaged in criminal behavior and you feel sorry enough for them that you believe you would try and diminish their detection, arrest or conviction at all costs, do yourself a favor and avoid this line of work so that you can avoid the embarrassment and the negative consequences that go along with it. Probably an even more vulnerable relationship frequently exploited is one involving romantic love.

A unique family member is your love interest. Significant others are kind of a combination of associates and family in that you chose them and then they became family or certainly like family. Moreover, who they are is important to prospective CRJ employers because generally speaking, more time is spent with significant others and they tend to have more influence on us than others. Recognizing this, it is essential for you to take note of those you involve yourself with on this level as it is highly likely husbands, wives, girlfriends and boyfriends will be scrutinized if you become the subject of a background investigation.

That choice you make of the person to spend most of your time with is viewed as significant enough to warrant scrutiny and permits others to form opinions about you. Your choice in a mate can identify how responsible you are; what you are willing to tolerate and what you are not willing to tolerate; and of course if you are talking about a situation where someone is engaged in illegal behavior – conclusions will be drawn about that as well. While you may be hoping for an illustration that you are a very compassionate person, a willingness to condone socially unacceptable behavior in a mate may be interpreted as irresponsible behavior. How it may be interpreted by a prospective CRJ employer, is that you may present more of a risk than what is acceptable for the position that you are applying for.

There will be consequences concerning your CRJ career for many choices you make from this point on. There are obvious situations you clearly must avoid if you wish to work in the field of criminal justice. But there are even more things that you will need to concern yourself with than just friends who have chosen another line of work. To some, the way things are may seem very restrictive and too much of a sacrifice. If this is you, recognize it early so that you do not spend too much time trying to get a degree in a field that you are not going to be comfortable working in. If much of what you have read thus far is not a problem for you – then go for it!

Life Application Exercise #1

To help you get in tune with the dynamics involved in how you and your employer might think about the topic of this section imagine this: You are visiting family, and at that very moment there is a raid at the house. The police come in with weapons and point them at you and instruct you to stay on the floor; they identify you; and then order you on the sofa where you have to sit until the raid is over because they find contraband in the house. How would you feel? Would you feel that it was worth it to spend time with people who have put you in jeopardy like that? How do you think your CRJ supervisor will react when you call and make such a notification to them?

Do you think that they are likely to understand? Or do you think this incident might present a problem? Add to this, the fact that your name ends up in the newspaper and a good investigative reporter attaches your work title to the byline making the story more juicy.

So what do you think about all of that? These are the things you must think about. I know it is easy to focus in on this as "not easy" or "unfair" and I will concede this to some extent. But it is the way things are. Are you willing to deal with reality? Are you an idealist or a realist? You certainly can be both on a situational basis. But involvement, no matter how brief in a situation such as the one presented, being overly idealistic or hoping that things are different is not going to help you deal with the reality of the situation.

Life Application Exercise #2

Much of our discussion on associations and friends involves common sense. When I was a teen I realized that I had a cousin who had sticky fingers. The first time a store security guard grabbed her when we left the store, I was very defensive and called her mother immediately complaining that she was being treated unfairly. However, after the second time, I concluded that she was a thief and realizing the possible peril she could put me in, I vowed never to go shopping with her again.

Think about relatives you have that you believe are involved in criminal offending. Do you believe that their activities could adversely affect your credibility or ability to work in the field of criminal justice if you closely associate with them? How so? Do you believe you should limit your association with these particular relatives? The good news is that you will not automatically be disqualified from a position simply because you have family members who have engaged in criminality, even if they are currently incarcerated. However, the question that will be raised is whether the family member currently criminally offends, and what is the nature of your relationship beyond familial ties. The answer can factor into whether you are viewed suitable to hold a criminal justice position. In other words, the focus is upon you.

Chapter 9

Loyalty

Are you more loyal to your friends or to your job's mission? What do you do when the two conflict? Your employer will expect you to be loyal to certain principles necessitating assurances as to how you will handle information obtained during the course of your work. Perhaps you will even be expected to take an oath of office to assert that you will uphold the guiding charter of the branch of government for which you will work, such as the U.S. Constitution if you become a federal worker.

The subject of loyalty involves all aspects of a CRJ position including within and outside of the agency. Some expression of loyalty will occur automatically without much thought on your part. However, you really discover who you are and how dedicated and loyal you are when you are forced to choose between two close relationships. So for our purposes, choosing loyalty between two extreme relationships will be explored. Since people are involved in many different relationships besides employer–worker, from time to time you may have to choose whether to be loyal to promises you made to your employer or to a friendship or other close relationship.

You are embarking upon a profession that will likely put you in much public contact which increases the likelihood that on at least one occasion your career will touch someone close to you. It is not far–fetched that during the course of your service as a criminal justice professional you will have to decide where your loyalties really lay—you will be called to the test. It may involve a potentially compromising situation involving learning something private and criminal about someone you know. The key to dealing with these situations is an overall guiding commitment and knowing yourself. You should already have settled in your mind and heart that should you ever encounter such a situation, you will come down on the right side. I have found the best practice is to inform the appropriate officials of the agency so that you may be extricated from the case to eliminate anyone later second guessing your decisions ranging from friends to co–workers.

Informing your boss about a potential problem affords you with insulation and an opportunity for your agency to plan how to minimize your involvement in a scenario that may have adverse consequences for you and the agency. If you are silent about a matter where you have uncovered potentially damaging information about an associate, your presence at the scene of adverse action (i.e. at an arrest or court hearing) may inflame the situation to a degree, that the so–called friends you think are so loyal to you may attempt to "save" their own hides by making up lies about your involvement in their criminal activities. Make no mistake about it, you as a criminal justice professional will always be viewed as a "bigger fish" than an ordinary criminal.[16]

But you may be thinking, what if you believe your friend or relative is incapable of doing what they have been accused of and is simply being "railroaded" by your agency. Again, my best recommendation is that you disclose immediately your association with the party in question. Working for the criminal justice system requires having some faith that those working in the system are capable of identifying the innocent as well as the guilty during its processes.

Life Application Exercise #1

What would you do if you found out through your work that one of your closest friends or a relative was about to be arrested? Your agency's plan was to arrest this friend in two days, raid their home, and seize

---

[16] I share this ideology. I believe it should be a priority of a criminal justice manager to root out undercover criminals posing as police, prosecutors, etc. within their ranks for effectiveness and to promote an image of being fair.

all valuable property suspected of being purchased with ill gotten gains.

It is important to note that an improper notification in the above scenario is not just poor conduct for a CRJ professional, but it is illegal to make such disclosures as well. One could be charged with obstruction of justice for tipping off others about impending law enforcement activity. Moreover, you could even face more extreme adverse actions such as being expected to make financial restitution for the value of the lost assets police had hoped to seize, that were not available as a result of an illegal leak of information.

Life Application Exercise #2

What would you do if asked by a close friend or relative to check out someone who is a potential mate – just so they can have "peace of mind" that the person is not a "triple–ax murderer". Get acquainted with what is forbidden at your CRJ agency and be ever mindful as to how your behavior is perceived by others. For example, your own attempt to learn more about a potential mate by accessing information in restricted databases at work may later be viewed as an attempt to inform him/her about anything you uncover versus to have fore–knowledge to make a decision. It would be a "which came first, the chicken or the egg" scenario and you would never be able to remove doubt cast on your motives even with a credible story especially if a breech of security is detected.

Life Application Exercise #3

Recently, I heard a news story (Friedman, 2003) about two brothers – one a prominent university president, the other a notorious criminal. Because the criminal brother was reported as a fugitive, the university president came under scrutiny as to his role in facilitating his brother's eluding the police. It is believed by some that the university president had contact with his brother that he refused to disclose.

Those in this camp sought the removal of the university president.[17]

If what is said about him is true, perhaps the university president wanted to help his brother—but the question becomes does he have a moral obligation to "harm" his brother? In looking at this situation you might view it from different angles. But an important question for the criminal justice major is whether you would be willing to do right by the job even if it will be viewed negatively by family.

What about you and this type of ethical dilemma? If it were your brother what would you do? There are legal requirements about harboring felons for example. Some relief in a situation such as this would be if you were to identify the whereabouts of the family member, you could at least have some involvement in the circumstances of capture—decreasing the likelihood of a violent climax. Probably the best example of this involved David Kaczynski's turning in his brother, Theodore Kaczynski, the infamous Unabomber who killed 3 people and injured over 20 in attacks involving bombings.

David Kaczynski has lectured and spoken publicly on his reasons for turning in Ted. David, a social worker having recognized similarities between a published manifesto and Ted's own ideas, turned him in to save innocent lives. "Brothers are supposed to protect each other and here I was, turning him in", David was quoted as saying during one seminar (Le, 2003) which leads to a conclusion that it probably was no easier for him to do this difficult thing than it would be for anyone else. Moreover, David has also reached out to the Unabomber's victims expressing his family's grief at the suffering endured (Harris, 1999).

---

[17] The university president later resigned amidst political pressure surrounding his fugitive brother and other issues (Kellogg, 2003).

Please keep in mind that regardless of the requisite obligations as a citizen on reporting, a law enforcement officer would have an obligation to report things such as this that others may not. An officer could be brought up on charges and subsequently dismissed for failure to report such information.

Chapter 10

Truth and Honesty

Did you know that as a criminal justice professional your "word" will be so revered that it may be used in affidavits to influence a judge to order a search and seizure warrant to raid someone's home, to cause the arrest of a person, or in some states in contributing to the ordered death of a convicted murderer? Based upon the nature of work for many CRJ professionals, your willingness to tell the truth must be uncompromising. Even telling "little white lies" is cause for concern for those working in an occupation that requires such a degree of honesty. Depending upon your position, in addition to preparing affidavits, you may have to testify in court (your expert opinion may even be sought out on a given matter) or give sworn statements.

Many CRJ professionals have the responsibility for gathering facts and analyzing them to come to some conclusion about an event or individual. And while you usually would not have the responsibility of being the ultimate determiner of truth (i.e. judge or jury), the outcome of your assessments may result in many adverse actions for others (i.e. degree of charges, arrest, conviction, etc.). These are serious matters. Consequently, those seeking to work in the criminal justice field should ponder whether they want a job with this degree of responsibility as well as judge their own ability to be accurate in their evaluations of people and circumstances.

Criminal justice professionals must battle any tendency to misrepresent facts, even if it will make them or their agencies look bad. After all, when it comes to some things where no corroboration is available, the truth of a matter may be determined solely on the CRJ practitioner's perspective or recollection of events. Under this circumstance, misrepresentations of fact cannot be proved, so it may be more tempting to skew things in your favor. Some have opted for the "I do not remember" account in an attempt to avoid revealing information which may help the other side. So the question becomes: if you tell a lie and no one knows or can prove it is a lie – is it still a lie? The answer is absolutely – yes, it is still an untruth. There is no known manner by which the truth may be extracted from a human so there is nothing that can be done to absolutely prove[18] that a lie was told. However, I do believe that the more one lies, the easier it becomes to repeat the behavior in the future – and one becomes well on his/her way of descending down the "slippery slope".[19]

Unfortunately, our society is uncovering more and more evidence to suggest that untruthfulness is more evident than many of us are comfortable with. An interview with Gregg Behr, Founding Director of Content of Our Character Project (Cooper, 2003) revealed that 93 percent of high school students surveyed reported lying at least once to their teachers and their parents. Moreover, 37 percent said they would lie to get a job.

I have found that telling the truth, even when it is uncomfortable is always the best practice – and frequently you will find that the expected consequence or negative outcome does not occur even when unpleasing information is revealed. The other thing about lies is that there always exists the possibility that they will be uncovered. This often leads to worry on the part of the person having told the lie. They then become distracted which of course can reflect negatively on their personal life and work performance. This is particularly poignant when one presents falsehoods as a basis for entry into the field of criminal justice.

The problem with lying to get the job is that you never know when the lie may be revealed. There is no apparent

---

[18] Although such a witness may be impeached if enough doubt may be cast on his/her credibility from the testimony of other witnesses.

[19] The concept of a slippery slope suggests that corruption is the result of a continuum where less serious compromises occur before more serious offenses.

statute of limitation on lying in that whatever the lie allowed you to get can also cost you it. In other words, if lying permitted you to get on the job—if the lie is detected, it can cost you the job later. Consider the following example:

"The Treasury Department tentatively selected Mary Brown[20] for employment with the Customs Service as a GS–7 Customs Inspector. But after her personal interview, the agency decided she was unsuitable for employment and rescinded its offer.

Brown's initial selection was subject to completion of all pre–employment requirements, including a background investigation. In her interview, she admitted using marijuana and cocaine and selling marijuana to friends 20 years ago as a teenager. She was denied the position.

Brown appealed and a judge found the misconduct as a juvenile was not sufficient to disqualify her. The judge ordered the agency to cancel its negative suitability determination. The agency then conducted an updated background investigation on Brown and found she had made false statements during the interview. It then issued a new negative suitability determination.

According to her application of a job with the Anaheim Police Department, Brown committed thefts when she was a teenager and again in her 20s. But she answered "no" when Customs asked if she was ever engaged in any criminal conduct that was not uncovered.

The agency stated that Brown had falsely answered "no" to the question of whether she was aware of any relatives who were involved in illegal activities—even though she and her brother were arrested together in 1978.

---

[20] Not real name included in case description. Mary Brown is substituted through this exert for the real name.

During the updated investigation, Brown told the investigator she had been fired in 1980 from a company. During the first investigation, however, she had falsely answered "no" to the question of whether she had ever been fired." —MSPB, SF073101044711, 9/30/03. (Federal Employees Digest, November 24, 2003).

Ultimately, the agency was able to convince decision makers (the Merit System Protection Board) that the candidate's falsification made her unsuitable for employment.

Not only will omission about negative information in your past create problems for your future, but exaggerating information can also prove detrimental. There is a situation that I still find hard to believe. It involved an exaggeration of a criminal justice professional representing himself as having previously worked for one branch of government, presumably because it was more prestigious in his viewpoint than the actual body of government that he did work for. It was the same position even, so I remain perplexed as to his decision to make this misrepresentation over and over again in sworn documents—which ultimately cost him his career. There are the omissions, exaggerations and then there is lying to facilitate misbehavior.

Withholding the truth to secure some benefit may be regarded as fraud. People lost their jobs for lying within months of my first appointment as a local police officer. When I was hired in 1978, the City of Detroit was very proactive in its effort to give consideration to persons receiving public assistance—but as it turned out even after hire by the police department as officers, some of these persons still continued to collect welfare although they were no longer eligible. I had crossed paths with a few of these officers and they did not seem like monsters. But as it turns out they were people who had not been truthful. Both the officers and the police department paid the price for this dishonesty; the officers with arrest and loss of their jobs, and the department with its reputation being tarnished.

Another example of an embarrassing act to an agency was recently reported concerning a single federal employee. That employee faces federal charges for theft of government vehicles owned by his agency during the terrorist attacks on September 11, 2001. He is accused of falsifying records of vehicles that were reported as damaged, destroyed or recovered to divert certain vehicles to be disposed of instead to his family members (Federal Employees News Digest, 2004).

Fraud is a relatively common crime where people who would not otherwise engage in criminality find themselves involved. You should be aware because it is a trap which can seriously adversely affect a criminal justice career. Decisions and actions that do not appear as a big deal at the time can turn out very serious. Fraud is one of those temptations that virtually everyone faces in their life. What I think makes them so enticing is that each fraud situation can be viewed as a solution to a problem. Consider in the examples below how easy it would be for someone to make a decision to engage in fraud that may have very bad consequences:

- The "lemon" that is not worth the payments you make every month. If only the car would be involved in an accident, burn up or disappear, the insurance company would pay it off – killing two birds with one stone: The car is paid for *and* gone, freeing up precious funds to buy another one.

- The misrepresentation that you live with your rich uncle to lower your insurance premiums and permit your children to go to a better school.

- Pretending sicker than you are stemming from a work related accident to receive more time off work, financial compensation, and other unmerited benefits.

- Fudging, just a little, on your taxes.

Worry and grief is associated with fraud. Fraud is the silent crime with many offenders never seeing themselves as criminals unless so labeled by the system when they are forced to reckon with their crimes. People who have engaged in fraud never know when the dirty deed might be exposed.

The aforementioned illustrations demonstrate just how important your word is a as a CRJ professional. But your word as one embarking upon a career in the field of criminal justice is just as important now as what you do today can affect your future. As a criminal justice major, you are embarking upon a certain career and it would be very disappointing for you to go through the trouble of all that work and then not be able to find the job that you have always desired or wanted to obtain.

I remember some years ago supervising an intern who was an excellent performer. I was very proud of this person's capabilities and felt that when he completed his studies in criminal justice that he was going to make a good law enforcement officer as it was his goal. I am not sure if he ever got the job he really wanted. You see, early in his college days, before he had reached the age of 21, he used a phony identification to purchase alcoholic beverages in a public place. He was caught, and documentation of this event was buried somewhere out there. When this intern successfully completed his internship and college studies, he started to seek employment with various law enforcement agencies; and he kept finding that he was not getting the job. If this incident was coming out each and every time, he could not say for sure. Nor could he attribute this event as the reason he was not being hired. But it vexed him enough that he contacted me and asked if I thought he should refrain from volunteering this information.

Many applications for law enforcement jobs contain questions about contact with police that are quite broad (expansive enough that this incident would fit into) and if one is not truthful, it probably would be used as a disqualifying factor during the selection process. So he was not getting a job, and the question he put forth to me was if he should stop being as forthcoming about the under–aged drinking citation; and I went on to explain to him that as bad as this situation may have seemed, it would be even worse if he lied about this event because he probably would end up in more trouble.[21]

You may be saying to yourself that he told the truth and he did not get the job, so what does he have to lose by *not* telling the truth. Well of course in the short term, one may very well end up getting *hired* for the job, but it does not necessarily mean that lying will help you *keep* the job. For example, one may have given conflicting statements to investigators for other positions applied for; however oftentimes other applications may be reviewed as well for consistency or discrepancies in responses, depending upon the position one is being investigated for. And even worse is that you may lose the job that you got—so as bad as it may be in not obtaining a job, just think about getting the job and maybe in training or even having started the job for a while and then losing it—being yanked off of a job because you were not truthful in your responses.

Evidence of dishonesty will most likely be a red flag for a prospective employer, but it should also be a red flag for you. A prospective employer's failure to hire you because its administrators feel that you will be a risk for the agency or that your personal ideology conflicts with its mission is not the worst thing that can happen to you. To me the worst thing that can happen to you is for a prospective employer to ignore these signs or for you to ignore tendencies at this stage and then to end up in a relationship—you and your employer together and something really bad happens. For one to succumb to some of these dishonest tendencies as a practicing CRJ professional could result in one facing criminal charges, and dismissal. Moreover, your employer may face some serious consequences if you are not truthful.

Scandal presents tough problems for any agency. Managers of the organizations where its employees have been

---

[21] It should be noted that even if this never rose to the level of an entry on a criminal rap sheet, campus police departments keep their own records about incidents involving students that are also frequently queried during the course of certain types of background investigations.

found to have been grossly dishonest become concerned about the level of embarrassment the agency will be subjected to. Moreover, what bearing is scandal going to have on the employees that remain? It is just a situation that is best avoided on the front end as opposed to having to deal with it on the back end. So remember, if you are tempted or inclined to want to make things look a certain way than the reality of the actual facts, not only can you affect the outcome of justice being served but you subject yourself and your employer to serious consequences.

This all means that you should strive for complete truthfulness in terms of what actually occurred. The stakes have become higher as our society studies lying more. Who one lies to and under what circumstances a lie is told can dictate situations from whether a person is allowed to retain a job to being criminally prosecuted.[22] There are even laws that have come out as a result of criminal court cases about defendant's rights. One of them is the Henthorn[23] decision which basically says that if there is a concern that your credibility has been an issue at work—whether that is a personnel issue, a previous case, or any bearing on your honesty, the defense has a right to know about it so if they choose to bring it up in court, they can. Again, any thing you have done in the past can have a bearing on your future. So your ability to be viewed as credible to some extent is based upon your ability to have been credible in previous circumstances. Whereas some employers would have previously been inclined to excuse behavior, it is now more apparent that employees with a credibility problem can seriously have an adverse impact on an agency's ability to carry out its functions and missions. CRJ agencies' ability to carry

---

[22] At the center of the charges filed against Martha Stewart is that she may have lied to authorities. From a CRJ ethics point of view the trial of Martha Stewart where she was convicted may become even more notorious for the alleged lies told by a CRJ professional. A government witness of the trial was recently charged with perjury surrounding his testimony about examination of forensic evidence (Farrell, 2004).

[23] Henthorn v. United States, 931 F.2d 29 (9th Circuit 1991).

out missions is based in large part on the conduct of their employees, especially with regard to them telling the truth.

Life Application #1

Think about some times when you have not been truthful. Think about the outcomes. I am confident that you will determine that while some outcomes were better than others—the fact that you can remember these falsehoods suggest that you were adversely affected even if no one else detected your untruthfulness. You probably have worried about these situations which alone is enough of a reason not to repeat them. Forgive yourself and move on. But do remember how this feels so you can endeavor to do better in the future. One last thought on this subject—if you find that you have told a lie where the consequences are so serious to you or others that you worry chronically, it may be time to seek professional help in either working through forgiveness or considering exposing the facts to the appropriate people.

Life Application Exercise #2

In a book entitled *The Day America Told the Truth*, (Patterson 1991), posed a question to determine what people would be willing to do for 10 million dollars. The results while startling,[24] were informative. Respondents in this study were permitted to remain anonymous. As has been demonstrated in research, I believe that when people are anonymous, they are more likely to be honest in their responses. Accordingly, participate in the exercise described below.

---

[24] Some results of this study were that varying percentages of the respondents said they were willing to murder a stranger, abandon their families, or undergo a sex change operation for a cool ten million.

If you are the person who facilitates this exercise, advise that no attempt will be made to identify the author. Prior to discussion, all participants, and there should be more than a few to ensure anonymity, everyone should be provided with a uniform card or piece of paper. Everyone should be instructed to type—ideally using the same font size for their response so they are comfortable that handwriting examination will not be an issue later. Everyone should be advised that being honest is as important to them as the rest of the group. The question to be posed is: "What is the most shocking thing you would be willing to do for 20 million dollars?"[25] The responses could be put in a box and mixed. A few should be pulled out and discussed as a group. This exercise will present you with a good idea of the norms of a given group as well as provide feedback to people about what others think about what they wrote. It is important to say again that a ground rule of this exercise should be that no attempt will be made to identify a participant. To further protect confidentiality on this exercise designed as realistic as possible, would be for various groups to swap their responses so that a given group is not working on its own responses.

Life Application Exercise #3

The name Pete Rose is probably now as famous for his baseball career as infamous for his lying about betting on baseball. It is unethical for professional baseball players to bet on baseball. Certain evidence suggested that Pete Rose had in fact bet on baseball during his professional career. However he had always denied that he had until early 2004 when he publicly admitted that he had in fact bet on baseball.

---

[25] I thought the ante should be increased to 20 million to account for inflation. After all, what one could obtain for 10 million a couple of decades ago, could not be acquired at the same amount(s) today.

Some seem to be as disappointed by the continual lying as about the betting. Now comes evaluations about Rose's "coming clean" in consideration of whether he will be permitted to work in some capacity with professional baseball. Although Rose had been censured already by prohibition to the Baseball Hall of Fame, do you believe his final revelation *should* or *will* change anything? Take time to answer both of these questions recognizing that part of the question is a judgment from you about whether his telling the truth *should* result in any different outcome; and your forecast of whether it will change anything is your belief about what the proper authorities will actually do.

How this inevitably turns out will illustrate many of the points discussed in this chapter. For one thing, just because one has an opinion about how a given matter should be handled, the decision–makers will use ethics of that profession to determine what really happens. Also, one can not permanently avoid consequences for the underlying behavior by lying; and even the lying itself carries its own distinct costs. Finally, the Rose situation is scandalous and has tarnished his reputation and that of baseball.

Conclusion

There are things that you have done in the past you obviously cannot go back and correct. But certainly there are things that you may have not thought would be issues, as it relates to your impending profession in the criminal justice field that you now know about. To the extent that becoming a criminal justice professional is a goal, you now know that you may need to make adjustments to your thinking and behaviors. Yes, you may know better who you are, but who you ultimately become is the important thing here. Forge into the next part of this book with a renewed sense of commitment knowing that you are preparing a foundation to succeed through the various screening phases to your new career in criminal justice!

Part III

The Selection Process

Chapter 11

What to Expect

You can write the greatest application; you can have the best resume; you can perform like no other candidate during an interview because you are a great orator – and all of this will have been in vain if you can not get through the final step which involves a background check with various screenings. If you cannot get over the final hurdle, there is a good chance that you will *not* get the job.

There are various screenings that you are likely to undergo in your quest for employment in the field of criminal justice. They include: urinalysis screening, fingerprinting and polygraph examination. Each screening is designed to build a sense of security with your prospective employer that you are being truthful. As intrusive as the current screenings are, I believe in the future we can expect more such as testing hair for drug use history.[26] I also predict that there will only be a matter of time before applicants for certain positions, probably to include law enforcement candidates will end up having to undergo some type of DNA testing in connection with a criminal history check.

This is probably the stage where you wonder what you have gotten yourself into. You may even be saying to yourself – why is it so important that they look at me like I am under a microscope? Well welcome to the world of criminal justice because it does not end at the background investigation – it *begins* there. It is a life where you are under constant scrutiny. Some of the screenings you will submit to prior to hire will continue to occur randomly such as urinalysis testing for certain jobs or on a cyclical basis such as a polygraph or background investigation. Still other testing

---

[26] Very recent (Geller, 2004) information released indicates that the federal government is planning to scrutinize employees' hair, saliva and sweat for drug screening purposes.

occurs if concerns about you develop or if you elect more sensitive assignments where another psychological or polygraph examination may occur beyond one required for initial candidate screening. Thus, if you are a very private person who will be uncomfortable with constant scrutiny, criminal justice may not be the best line of work for you because others may frequently get in your business and even judge your actions.

Think for a moment about the power that you will wield – whether you are in law enforcement, corrections, probation, or prosecution. All of these positions are of power where you have authority to make decisions about whether people will go free, or whether they will be imprisoned and for how long. Some jobs such as police officer empower one to take a life in the line of duty if necessary. When you have that kind of authority, responsibility and discretion at your hand, it is very important that you can exercise sound judgment. Therefore, it is very important that you can be trusted and depended on to make critical decisions. This is much of the reason why you are subjected to so much scrutiny.

Getting a job in law enforcement is more than filling out an application and an interview. It is those things too, but it also involves your entire life—things that you have done up until the point that you apply for the job. Because of the trust that is eventually placed in your hands, for this coveted occupation, employers feel that it is very important that they select people who are psychologically sound. Folks who are able to make sound judgments – people who are able to demonstrate based on their past behavior that they *can* and *will* make sound judgments. Your background will be scrutinized to such an extent that you never thought possible.

Things that you have done up to this point are certainly important, but things that you do for the four years that you are in college in pursuit of a criminal justice degree or in a police academy possibly are even more important, because these things are viewed in a different context. A person who knows he or she is interested in the CRJ profession, and in spite of this still makes poor decisions is viewed more harshly. For example, experimentation with drugs or getting phony identification to purchase alcohol are unwise things to do; however, when viewed from the context of someone who at the *time* these things were done knew in fact that they for example wanted to enforce the law—it would be viewed very differently. It is more damaging because now here is a judgment issue where one could conclude that a person making these kinds of poor choices while majoring in CRJ is indicative of not caring about where it may lead. It could be that the person was just oblivious to the fact that their personal life is going to viewed that way, but the result may still be the same (ignorance is no excuse).

Surviving the various stages of the hiring process for a criminal justice position can depend upon your stamina and patience. In developing your endurance, it helps to know what to expect and some of the reasons why your prospective employers will appear so nosey. Agencies, as they should, invest a lot of time, energy and money in selecting the right people for the job. Failure to do so can be catastrophic. All it takes is one individual to tarnish the reputation and effectiveness of a criminal justice agency. As will be discussed further, some police departments have been subjected to external monitoring because of a few officers' having violated the civil rights of the citizens they were charged to protect.

This part is in three sections and provides you with identifying important tests that you cannot study for. Although the polygraph, psychological assessment and background investigation each tests you in some way, who you have become will determine whether you pass these critical tests. That is why it is never too early to get into "ethical shape." It is a state of mind which needs to be developed and refined early in life.

Chapter 12

"Getting High: Not in the Job Description"[27]

(Drug Use –To Use or Not to Use?)

In writing this, I found there was this section of information that did not neatly fit into the outline. It involves an issue in the life of a young person that may not have been settled or decided upon as yet — but important all the same. It involves the issue of drug use that if uncovered during a background investigation and viewed as derogatory will eliminate any chance of a criminal justice career. Although many who have used drugs will tell you that they decided impulsively and were not really thinking, you must take all aspects of your future, including your suitability for hire into consideration when making this important decision.

A decision to experiment in drug use could potentially affect your goal to work in the criminal justice system more than any other. Far and foremost, experimentation in drug use can lead to drug addiction. And any drug addiction will limit your ability to work in many criminal justice positions and probably eliminate any opportunity to work as a law enforcement officer completely.

---

[27] This subtitle was inspired by a video tape advertisement for a tape entitled "Getting High: Not in the Job Description." The advertisement in the Fall, 2003 Abuse, Addiction & Recovery catalog (Cambridge Educational) suggests that "whether you work on an assembly line in a factory or write computer programs for a company's accounting department, you have a right to a safe and drug–free work environment. This program is designed to help viewers of all ages understand their rights and responsibilities on the job, to increase their protection from coworkers whose critical thinking and decision–making skills may be impaired through substance abuse."

The reasons for this are obvious in that law enforcement officers are exposed to narcotics on a regular basis during the course of discharging their duties. If someone has developed an "appetite" for drugs, it would be fool–hearty for the addict or the law enforcement agency to take the risk not to consider that a routine assignment involving drugs could lead to a relapse on the part of the individual; and all of the negatives for the agency from prosecution jeopardy for the investigation to ensuing scandal(s).

It could be that you know of someone who has used drugs and after getting help they were able to move on in life, so you do not see where drug use presents a major problem. However, you need to be mindful that even if these are things one has worked through, the eyes of the beholder in this instance will be an employer. A criminal justice administrator may believe that drug use is serious enough that this issue is intolerable for its workforce. While an employer may be sympathetic, certain CRJ employers will be less concerned about your ability to have survived, dealt with, or overcame a particular issue and instead more concerned about temptations and your susceptibility to corruption. The bottom line is drug addicts and people using beyond experimentation will find it hard (if not impossible) to obtain professional employment in the field of criminal justice.

What is drug experimentation? At what point does trying out a drug become viewed as drug use, abuse or even addiction? Answering this question from a medical viewpoint is beyond the scope of my abilities, but what I can say from the perspective of a CRJ executive is that anything beyond trying something once, but no more than twice to me is an indication that the person enjoyed the drug. To take it a step further, if they enjoyed the drug there is every reason to believe that they continued use, probably abused and maybe even became addicted. I recognize that my perspective is subjective, however, CRJ executives across the nation many, of which are as conservative as I am, base their decisions on similar rationale. The real question that many applicants want the answer to is: "how many times can I use a particular drug before I become disqualified?" Now I

want to believe that those posing the question are concerned about whether it is already too late for them versus
trying to figure out how much they can do in the future. Because my best advice to you is that if you have never experimented with drugs, then never choose to do so.

I have taken to gathering data informally whenever the
subject of drug use comes up. People who contend that they
have never used drugs before are able to articulate how
they were able to avoid using and do so with conviction. I
have never used drugs. Having made up my mind at an
early age that I never wanted to try them, and on those few
occasions when I was a teen and marijuana was discussed, I
made my stance perfectly clear to others and I left if the
drug was produced. It did not take long before everyone
knew and seemed to respect my decision. Conversely, people who represent that they have never used drugs before
and yet they have used drugs, seem to have a difficult time
with that question. And I have found that their hesitation
in responding to questions about drug use leads to an ad-
mission that they had in fact at least experimented. I believe the reason for the hesitation is that one can not
articulate well the absence of an experience if it in fact did
occur.[28]

I am not naïve enough to think that the choice to not use
drugs may be a hard one for some. I recently came across an
article about a parent giving advice to other parents about
the extent to which they should be truthful with their children about drug use. One of the inferences in the article was
the sense it was hard to avoid drugs, especially at social
gatherings where apparently drugs, especially marijuana,
is frequently on the scene. I reflected about the parties I
have attended. I concede that I am not a "social butterfly,"
but at these gatherings I attended, I did not see drugs there.
I would suggest to you that if every party that you attend,

---

[28] What you need to understand from this is that presenting falsehoods about drug use to trained investigators will likely result in
the truth being discovered anyway and now you will have to contend with a lie being told which can have more far–reaching consequences than drug experimentation.

drugs are there, you are not going to the right parties; or you are socializing with the wrong types of people. Granted, based on my experiences in the 1970s, drug use seemed less prevalent than now. So how does one in the twenty first century avoid drugs?

I think the key to drug use avoidance is vigilance. Not only should parties where drug use is occurring be avoided,[29] if you find yourself someplace where people are discussing the issue freely and intimately, they should be avoided as well—because even if no drugs are present, it is probable that those discussing previous or planned drug use are engaging in a lifestyle that is contrary to a lifestyle a CRJ major should pursue. Parties where drugs are being consumed, even if you do not partake, should be avoided for another reason.

Certain positions in criminal justice require you to submit to a urinalysis screening, and if you are attending a party where marijuana is being smoked, even if you are not smoking it, you may ingest it on a second–hand basis. This indirect ingestion may result in your becoming intoxicated on some level and depending on the concentration and how much of it gets into your system you could test positive for the presence of marijuana in your body. A positive drug test during a urinalysis screening will likely disqualify you from hire for a CRJ job you are seeking and put any job that you already have at risk for dismissal. And what a dreadful thing to be dismissed for. It places one in a situation to be "black–listed" where finding subsequent employment in the field of criminal justice is virtually impossible absent extreme deception. When you are seeking employment in the field of criminal justice you are frequently expected to disclose all current and past employers—and your reason for leaving those positions. Moreover, frequently, past su-

---

[29] I am not the only law enforcement officer to take this approach. Retired FBI Special Agent Johnnie Gibson Bright (2003) declares in her memoir during her single days when she attended parties as soon as she saw partygoers using drugs she would have to leave.

pervisors and co-workers are interviewed and personnel files reviewed during background investigations.

A decision to interact with drug users can put a criminal justice position at peril, as much as a decision to use drugs. Some feel that just because they themselves are not using drugs, being with someone who does is not problematic. However, what you must consider is that unbeknownst to you, associating with those who use drugs may put you right in the middle of their activities. For example, they may engage in criminal behavior to try and obtain funds to purchase the drugs that they use. Moreover, possession of illicit drugs is a crime in every state for just about every drug.

The fact that drug possession is a crime means that you may be arrested resulting in an entry onto a criminal record. Any arrest, whether for a misdemeanor or a felony is usually disclosed when seeking employment in law enforcement, and is likely noted during background investigations. Will an arrest for smoking a joint automatically eliminate all possible prospects in the field? Probably not—but who needs the aggravation and concern associated with it.

Even if experimental or recreational drug use does not lead to addiction or arrest, undoubtedly, it can lead to malevolent associations. People who sell drugs are not the kind of associations criminal justice administrators have expectations that their employees will associate with. Moreover, associating with drug dealers bring on all kinds of problems such as anytime you are in their company is "being in the wrong place"—drug dealers are subject to arrest at any time by police not to mention robbery or assault by competing criminal elements. Any of this kind of "drama" in your life, while not necessarily involving official action may be enough to cause a potential employer to look elsewhere to someone lacking such a provocative past.

The other thing that you should be wary of is not getting in the middle of a drug deal. Lets say you are somewhere and one person asks you to hand something to another person. If you agreed, you would be right in the middle and could possibly be viewed as facilitating—this is especially bad if caught and you are the one possessing the drugs. So friends who use drugs; places you go where drugs are being used—avoid at all costs anything along these lines, because otherwise, you may end up with some bothersome concerns which you just as well could do without. As previously mentioned, a drug conviction can even affect your ability to obtain a degree in criminal justice, or any other field for that matter based on the federal ban for giving federal aid to college students (Levinson, 2001).[30]

The issue of drugs will be revisited in the next section on background investigation. The distinction between this section and the next is that this was an attempt to dissuade those who have never experimented with drugs from ever doing so, while the next section provides insight on the process and how it may be for those who have already used drugs.

Life Application Exercise

Ask yourself these questions concerning drug use: Can it lead to addiction? Can it lead to arrest? Can it lead to associations which may interfere with my ability to get a CRJ job?

---

[30] However, there has been some sympathy towards first or second time offenders in that their criminal records often prohibit them from obtaining employment. The Second Chance commission (Koch, 2000) of New York State developed the Second Chance Program that in certain cases provides for sealing criminal records permitting these offenders to lawfully respond "no" to questions on job applications about ever being convicted of a crime. However, criminal records remain available for those seeking jobs in law enforcement. In other words, if you have been convicted of a felony, it is unlikely you will get a job in this field.

Chapter 13

The Background Investigation: Getting to Know Who You Are

The primary purpose for a background investigation is for your prospective employer to get to know who you are. The bottom line on most background inquires is that your prospective employer needs to establish some degree of confidence that you can be trusted. Previous indicators of mistrust are likely indicators that trusting you may be risky. Some agencies are willing to take more risk than others. But you will find that the most prestigious, competitive and sought after positions are those where employers are less willing to take risks on candidates.

The good news is that if you make it to this stage it is a positive indicator that you are being seriously considered for the job as a background investigation can be costly. Thus many CRJ agencies reserve this procedure for only those candidates they are close to hiring. It really is the last assurance that they are seeking of what is hoped as a good decision in choosing you. In this quest for getting to know you better, a background investigator will consider multiple sources to put together information which is like a puzzle. Your history is checked from many different angles. In short, investigators will get into "your business."

You may also ask yourself how these criminal justice agencies are permitted to be so nosy. But you must keep in mind that you are seeking positions of great authority where your ability to exercise sound judgment can not be understated. Depending upon your position you may have the authority to arrest or prosecute people. Moreover, if you become a law enforcement officer, if it becomes necessary you will have the authority to use deadly force that may re-

sult in death of another. We know that more is generally required from those who have been entrusted much,
especially in the way of authority. Such is the case with the
prestigious positions in the field of criminal justice.

Still, while you may be comfortable with why agencies
may determine they need to know so much about you, you
may ask how they can pry like this. After all, do you not
have a right to privacy in this country? This is true for certain things like the *Right to Financial Privacy Act* which legally prohibits intrusions into many financial transactions
or other private records you are associated with. However,
many protected institutions are queried with your consent.
Agencies that require background checks most likely will
request that you sign release documents that give your permission in advance for them to delve into your past. Your
refusal to sign any such waiver is likely viewed as a signal
that you have something to hide. Moreover, you are likely to
be disqualified as a candidate since a condition of hire is the
background investigation, which is predicated upon an
ability to check into areas requiring a signed release from
candidates to obtain confidential information. You can exercise your right not to waive these rights – but the question
you must ask yourself is if this decision will cause you to
gain or lose the job you want.

You should also take note that this is likely only the
start of your CRJ employer's intrusion into your life, as
some positions require periodic updated investigation during the course of your entire career. There are even times
when an investigation is launched outside of the regular cy-
cle if there is an integrity violation complaint made against
you. Thus, if you are a very private person who does not like
others looking into your life, you really should reconsider
criminal justice as an occupation source.

It has been established why CRJ employers will need to
conduct a background investigation. This section will now
focus on *where* they will look for clues about who you are,
what they are looking for and what this all is likely to mean
to you.

Driving record

Many criminal justice positions require you to drive a work vehicle. To that end, your driving history/record may play a part in the decision–making for hire. If you have a history of many traffic infractions, it may adversely affect your ability to obtain employment as you are viewed as an unacceptable risk. Moreover, if you have any history of driving while under the influence, you increase the possibility of being denied employment, especially if you are expected to drive a work vehicle.

Drinking and driving is viewed not only as negative by our society,[31] but also by conservative employers. A criminal justice employer may determine that conduct such as this is a major sign of poor judgment. As one expected to investigate, enforce, and uphold the law, breaking it is seriously frowned upon. This is one subject I feel compelled to weigh in on as far as providing examples of terrible situations I personally know[32] about.

We all know that drunk or drugged driving[33] can lead to serious accidents which may lead to critical injury or even death. But I am also aware of other tragedies involving alcohol and criminal justice employees—like the drunk federal agent who after waking up in the car of a fellow agent who was transporting him home pulled his gun and shot his co–worker dead. Not only did he lose his job, but he served time after he was convicted of charges related to killing the

---

[31] In fact, it is viewed so negatively that at least one state has initiated a unique labeling system. Effective January 1, 2004, Ohio drivers arrested on DUI charges and given special driving privileges will be required by law to use a yellow license plate with red numbers (Hull, 2003).

[32] Some agencies even place their personnel on call which has implications for the employee that may be too inebriated to respond to an unexpected field emergency.

[33] Less reported but still a serious problem is the driving while drugged. In fact one study suggested that more than half of the prople admitted to a Shock–Trauma Center after auto accidents tested positive for illegal drugs (Hartley, 2003).

other agent. Then there was the federal agent who woke up the morning after a night of drinking who went to his car and observed blood and other matter on the exterior. Concluding that he had killed a pedestrian, he committed suicide. It was later determined that he had ran over an animal. Is this terrible stuff or what? Each of these incidents point to the fact that criminal justice professionals and those intending to enter the profession should avoid getting drunk—period. And never, never drink excessively and drive.

As I write this, another public example of how drunk driving can adversely affect a criminal justice career and agency came to the fore–front. Although the case currently is at the charging stage, in the early morning hours of New Year's Day, 2004 the Chief of the Transportation Security Administration (TSA) at Dulles International Airport was arrested for drunk driving. As bad as the fact of a TSA Director being arrested for drunk driving seems and the fact the nation was at a Code Orange Alert at the time; add to this that a spokesperson for TSA said that at the time of the arrest, the Director "should have been participating in a security exercise to ensure the safety of air travelers at that hour" (Ginsberg, 2004). Although the TSA Chief had prior law enforcement experience[34] before taking that job, I daresay the drunken driving experience may affect his future prospects in the field.

Careless or reckless driving are also signs of irresponsibility that can result in accidents and may have consequences on a CRJ career. A good example of how one's driving history can adversely affect a life and career involves the recent conviction of Congressman William Janklow for vehicular manslaughter and other charges. Congressman Janklow's driver's history demonstrated a reckless disregard for obeying speed limits. Moreover, he publicly joked about his speeding escapades prior to the accident. This history was introduced in court at the trial which likely played a part in jury deliberations. Not only

---

[34] Schneider (2004) reports that Charles Brady, the arrested official, is a Secret Service Agent.

did this tragedy affect the family of the deceased, it also ended the Congressman's career—he announced his intention to resign the same day he is scheduled for sentencing. A commitment to drive responsibly can protect you in many ways.

Minor traffic infractions are generally not enough to create any serious problems for you; however, if you have encountered any episodes such as drunk driving, or having your license suspended, it is considered a red flag. It is the kind of thing that will cause a prospective employer to at least reconsider whether you are the right person for the job. One with this kind of baggage may hope that the agency will take a chance on him or her. However, from the eyes of the employer, such people are probably viewed as a risk or liability; and with so many people competing for a small number of jobs, disqualifying, especially if there is an expectation of operating an official vehicle in performance on the job.

Even if your job does not require you to drive an official vehicle, your driving record may be reviewed because it helps in putting together the puzzle pieces concerning who you are. The bottom line on a search and check of your driving history is that it helps to assess how responsible you are and determine whether you are eligible to operate an official vehicle if it is necessary.

Life Application Exercise

What conclusions would you draw about a person whose driving record exposed three tickets for speeding in the past year and one driving while intoxicated resulting in a conviction where there was no accident involved? Would that affect your decision to hire the person even if they would not need to operate a work car?

Money

Probably one of the best ways of determining your dependability is review of your credit history. Your record on whether you made good on the promises you made to creditors demonstrates if you are a person of your word. If and how you pay back monies you have borrowed is definitely a source of review during any background investigation. At minimum, expect a check into your credit history. What will your credit report say about you?

In reviewing your credit history, many CRJ agencies just want to ensure that you have satisfied your debts—regardless of how close that may have been to submission of your application for employment. However, I personally defer to selection of persons who have already established a pattern of "doing the right thing" regardless of whom is watching. In other words, if getting a good job is the only true motivation for paying your bills (and the monies were obviously available to make the payments) this may present a concern to some employers. I admit that I may be more conservative than the average CRJ administrator on this issue and it is likely due to a personal experience.

Without taking into consideration how it would affect my ability to get a job, when I was in between law enforcement jobs (I had been laid off from my first law enforcement job and had yet to be hired by a second law enforcement agency), I sent letters to my creditors explaining my situation. In the letters I promised to pay them once I obtained employment and when I did, although it took a while because I was not making as much money as I had when I secured the credit, I paid each creditor back. When it came time for my background investigation in my current job (the third law enforcement agency I worked for), the subject of my credit came up because one of the creditors still had posted that I had not satisfied the debt; however, having saved my payment receipts,[35] I was able to demonstrate that I had. Now I do not know for sure what would have happened if I had not paid these creditors, but I did not have to worry about that nor was I adversely affected. I paid these creditors back not because I even remotely thought it would affect my ability to get work in the field but because I owed the money. If you ever find yourself in a situation where you fall on hard times, develop a plan and chip away at the debt as soon as you are able to. It will look much better than appearing to have ignored the problem.

If you pay back creditors as agreed, you send a message to prospective employers and others that you can act responsibly. However, the reverse is also true in that if you do not pay your bills or continuously pay them late, without cause, you may be interpreted as irresponsible and untrustworthy. College loans present a point of reference on many former student's credit reports. If you default on your student loans (or any loan) not only is there the responsibility issue, but you may also appear ungrateful as these funds were provided to help you obtain your college degree, permitting you to qualify for work in certain criminal justice positions.

Some credit problems seem a product of over–extension. Unfortunately, today college students are bombarded with opportunities to obtain credit. Therefore, it is not unusual for students to graduate from college without a job having already amassed substantial debt beyond college loans. Remember, debt is an easy thing to get into and a hard thing to get out of. And right out of college, it is challenging enough to re–pay college loans without the high interest rates you face on credit cards for goods you may think you need. But recognizing that upon graduation, you may not have much of an income, all that debt is harder to manage. With my sit-

---

[35] I recommend that you keep very good records especially if you end up in a situation where you have to pay someone slower than agreed or if you have to pay a collection agency. Maybe the creditor promised to take it off your credit report—maybe they will and maybe they will not. But you do not want to rely solely on the creditor who may have felt wronged to "clear" your name. You need to ensure that you have copies of your canceled checks, and receipts. Keep your own files so you can demonstrate that a particular debt was satisfied should it ever come up.

uation, it really helped that the debt I had to repay was not substantial enough to be over–whelming. As you accept credit cards and use them without employment, know that an inability to re-pay may have adverse consequences on more than future credit.

One thing to consider is just how much debt you have. Is your debt in line with your income? To one reviewing a credit report from any perspective, it really looks bad if you have excessive debt and there is absolutely no way that you will be able to keep up with those payments. In other words, living from paycheck to paycheck[36] can be problematic. For example having to rely on loan–shark[37] type financial services is a sign that your finances may be unbalanced. The big question of overextension is how are you going to make repayment? The job that you are trying to get may have a better income than the one you have, but it still may not be enough money to help you keep this debt at a manageable level. And while having extensive debt is not illegal or unethical, it may be the kind of thing that certain CRJ employers strive to avoid in candidates as there is no desire to tempt anyone into corruption. Remember you may be competing with many other people even at the background stage.

Too much debt in relationship to income is also probably one of the most common reasons for entering into bankruptcy. While bankruptcy may be the clearest indication that a person's finances are completely a mess, it will not necessarily disqualify you from getting a job in criminal justice. Just because one files bankruptcy or a form of bankruptcy does not mean that you would not be able to obtain a

---

[36] Although I recognize that this is the American way, what I'm talking about here is that there is not even enough paycheck to cover the existing debt.

[37] I heard about this on the radio when I worked in New York. These "creditors" will loan you money until you get your next paycheck and then you can pay it back with some kind of interest. It is sort of an advance, but not in the true sense because there is interest to pay. To me, for one to enter into this type arrangement, there exists some level of desperation.

public service position in the field of criminal justice. There was a time when bankruptcy was frowned upon more because it was less common. And just as I indicated in the introduction that a lessened pool of candidates who do not make a standard, often means that standards will be lowered to ensure there are persons for hire. I believe that due to the fact that it has become more common for persons to have financial woes, there has been a lowering of standards in this area by CRJ agencies.

Still one must factor in what a bankruptcy may say to a prospective employer about how responsible and dependable you are. It is likely that the circumstances of the bankruptcy are evaluated. Was it just a total demonstration that one did not care as evidenced in running up a lot of spending and debt and then bailing out via bankruptcy? Or was it a situation where there may have not been an ability to handle a hardship any other way resulting from crises such as the loss of a job that they had for a long time, or the death of someone in the family who contributed significantly to the family's income? Obviously all circumstances are not created equal and if you do have evidence of a poor credit history, expect to have to document it in an explanation letter which details your particular situation.

Aside from your credit report, another aspect of your financial history which may come up during a background investigation is how you handle your checking account. There is a very thin line between the irresponsible behavior of repeatedly bouncing checks and the illegal behavior of passing bad checks. Lets say you "floated" several checks, gambled and lost. So now you have all of these fees you have to pay and even had your bank decline to permit you a checking account which clearly indicates that at least one outside entity has declared you as irresponsible. Intentional or not, a history of writing checks that do not clear the banking system may result in a derogatory financial history which may come to the attention of a prospective employer. There are all kinds of ways that bad check writing may be contained in records from being officially charged to a cross—link to a credit record to a co—worker or associate making the disclosure during background interviews. Will this prevent you from getting the job? Again, it depends on the severity and your ability to provide a satisfactory explanation.

Another area of financial concern may be child support payments. Many institutions are willing to garnish wages of parents who do not make court–ordered child support payments. Failure to financially support one's children, especially when you can is probably the most illustrative sign of irresponsible behavior. Yes, this can affect your ability to obtain a CRJ position.

Since the criminal justice system is driven by public institutions, you are likely to work for the federal, state or local governments directly or indirectly. Consequently, depending on your geographic area, taxes may be collected by the same governmental body that you work for. It is reasonable to assume that any evidence to evade paying taxes to any body of government you have a responsibility to pay will not only likely cause legal action, but also may adversely impact your ability for hire by that government. Payment of taxes is a civil responsibility.

If you just think about your life as one big field of responsibility, it may present you with identifying opportunities in your life to handle things in a manner that you will feel proud of, and viewed positively by prospective employers. It is not enough to focus on the negative side that a failure of financial responsibility can cause you not to get a job, but also focus on the positives of how much more you will accomplish in addition to getting a good job, if you are financially responsible. If you demonstrate that you are a responsible person, it will help in convincing the right people that you are someone who can be trusted with the responsibility of one of the most serious positions in our nation – that of the criminal justice professional.

Criminal history

Shoplifting is stealing! It's not a prank, a joke or a thrill. It's a crime. Even if it's your first offense, you could be punished with up to $2,000 in fines and five or more years in prison, *plus a record that could haunt you for the rest of your life*. We prosecute shoplifters. Please don't risk it! (1997 Wal*mart Stores, Inc.)

I recently observed the above caption on a sign inside of the stall door in a bathroom at a Wal*mart Store. I thought that this warning yelled as loud as I am attempting to yell throughout this book. "Plus a record that will haunt you for the rest of your life" is as real as it gets. Once you are arrested for anything, there is a good chance that it will remain in a system of records indefinitely. What that means is that any CRJ employer that will consider hiring you will always have access to the information that you were arrested. Your arrest is marked by the taking of your fingerprints which will also present a means by which the information about your arrest is accessed regardless of whether your name changes. This is an important thing to know because even agencies that may not require an extensive background investigation, at minimum will check to see if you have a criminal record and send off a copy of your fingerprints to the Federal Bureau of Investigation for comparison before hiring you.[38]

What gets included on a criminal record? Generally any arrest, whether for a misdemeanor or a felony and any con-

---

[38] I came across an amusing story relevant to this subject in <u>America's Dumbest Criminals</u> (1995): "Several years ago in Arkansas, a man robbed a pharmacy clerk at knife point. A few days later, the clerk picked the man out of a photo lineup and pressed charges against him. When the case went to trial, however, the man was nowhere to be found. He had fled the state, and officials had no clue where. They knew he came from New York City, but couldn't be sure that was where he had gone, and they didn't know where in New York to look. They really didn't have much hope of catching him. Then they got the break they needed to find

viction of an offense will be included on a criminal record. Crimes are classified into felonies and misdemeanors, with felonies being viewed as the more serious of the two. Most criminal justice agencies are not likely to hire those with felony convictions unless of course the felony has been expunged or excused in some other legal way.[39] But generally speaking, if one has a felony conviction, it will disqualify him or her from being able to get many criminal justice positions. So basically, arrests and convictions for the serious crimes of murder, aggravated assault, robbery, rape, grand larceny, automobile theft or arson will prohibit you from being able to engage in employment in the field of criminal justice. A conviction for one crime regardless of whether it is classified as a felony can automatically disqualify a candidate from becoming a law enforcement officer anywhere in the United States.

Under the Lautenberg Amendment to the Federal Gun Control Act, it is a federal crime for law enforcement officers to possess a firearm or ammunition, including service weapons, if they have been convicted of a state misdemeanor charge of domestic violence.[40] Thus if you are a law enforcement officer, and you are convicted of even a misde-

---

their criminal. Sure enough, the suspect had returned to New York and had applied for a job. Federal authorities were alerted when the man's prints were sent to Washington, D.C., as part of a standard check required for that particular job application. The man was soon arrested, charged, and convicted. Oh, and he didn't get the job he applied for—that of police officer."

[39] Even an expungement is not a guarantee that records are not available to criminal justice agencies. A recent BJS (2003) report containing the results of policies/practices of state criminal history repositories regarding modification of felony convictions found that 24 states have statues that provide for the expungement of records. However, only 11 of the states actually destroy the record. The situation is even bleaker for those attempting to conceal pardons in that the same study found that while all 50 states have statutes for the granting of pardons, in 45 states and the District of Columbia the criminal history record is retained with the action noted.

[40] Title 18, U.S.C., Section 922(g)(9).

meanor for domestic violence, you could lose your job.[41] Moreover, those seeking employment in the field of policing should know that the law applies to convictions before and after its effective date of September 30, 1996, (U.S. Department of Justice, 1998) meaning past behavior may already restrict your employment in the field of criminal justice.

In short, this is a rare situation where the people already hired and prospective candidates trying to get their foots in the door were almost in the same boat. "Almost" because the approach for some agencies when this legislation was pending enactment was to afford their officers with felony or misdemeanor convictions for domestic violence, to attempt to get their convictions pardoned or reduced in some manner. But what if you are now trying to get a job in law enforcement and you have a misdemeanor or felony conviction for this type of assault? Most agencies would not see a benefit in trying to permit a candidate to fix the situation (i.e. getting the conviction set aside) when there are candidates who do not have this baggage. The bottom line concern is that due to evidence of violence, one convicted of domestic violence should not carry a firearm. Whereas before one with a misdemeanor conviction for domestic violence could have been considered and got the job, after the law took effect this factor alone would make those with convictions seem less desirable for highly competitive jobs meaning they would have a high probability of being screened out. This is a very important matter that you should ensure is not a problem or issue for you, especially if law enforcement is the CRJ career you have chosen. Also keep in mind that even criminal justice jobs that do not require you to carry a firearm, do require sound judgment.

Even within the range of misdemeanor crimes, some are regarded more serious than others and may be treated as felonies for purposes of hire. For example, while classified as a misdemeanor, a malicious destruction of property con-

---

[41] This law is gender neutral. While many arrested for domestic violence are male offenders, I am aware of a case where a person lost their job as a result of a domestic violence arrest involved a female law enforcement officer.

viction that demonstrated a serious level of maliciousness may result in disqualification. Also crimes committed that were felonies and later pleaded down to a misdemeanor could also create a suitability problem. Background investigators may consult arrest reports as well as any other information to clarify what occurred in order to reach a determination as to whether it has bearing on one's level of responsibility, judgment, or future offending.

It remains a criminal act in the United States to possess most illicit substances. And even where marijuana possession in user quantities is not a felony, it is a misdemeanor which may result in an entry onto a criminal record. Any arrest, whether for a misdemeanor or a felony is a requested disclosure when seeking employment in law enforcement and is likely noted during background investigations. Will an arrest for smoking a joint automatically eliminate all possible prospects in the field? Probably not—but the aggravation and concern associated with it is a nuisance.

There are things out there that are not even classified as crimes yet. Laws are constantly being passed by various legislative bodies. An example of this was when steroid usage became illegal over–night. People who had used steroids on one day, could not legally do so in this country on the next day. Moreover, even if there are crimes on the books there are trends as to when and how they will be enforced. This is why it is important for a CRJ candidate to know the difference between right and wrong as it can save you heartache later. A good example is what occurred with the music industry's decision to seek action against those perceived to have illegally downloaded music from the internet. Although many of these cases are being handled civilly, there is the potential for criminal action. What you need to ask yourself is how will a prospective employer—especially a conservative employer view conduct such as this? Also remember that it does not take much to be put out of the race for a job during the screening process. The only thing needed is for employers to identify applicants more qualified and in some cases less troublesome than you to screen you out.

Doing right can save you when something is illegal and you do not know it is illegal. Consider the example of a school teacher in New York (New York Post, 1999) who probably did not believe that what she did was illegal, but certainly should have thought it wrong. It resulted in serious consequences for her. What she did was to use her daughter's student identification in order to get a cheaper rate on her fare instead of the one she should have used which was an adult pass. As a result of using the student pass, she ended up having an intervention with the law. There was a detention by the local port authority and she was arrested on theft charges. Moreover, pursuant to her arrest for theft, drugs were found on her person. Suffice it to say, she had a pretty bad day. But again, she probably did not think that what she did would result in such severe consequences.

Short of arrest, sometimes people have contact with police that result in temporary detection. These detentions often are the result of "being in the wrong place at the wrong time." Perhaps you are with friends, they do something and you are not involved, but until the police can sort it all out you are taken into custody. Say they question you, they realize you are not involved and you are released. However, some police departments, at college campuses in particular keep records of detentions or a notation of the police contact. There might even be some incident report filed. If you live in a college dorm, for example, and there is some type of an incident, there may be a record. Security officers at establishments or businesses often document incidents which may find their way into a background investigation. Depending upon if it is revealed there is documentation available at a certain place to bear witness to your character about something that has occurred. And keep in mind that background investigators are interested in patterns. So if you have multiple instances of the same kinds of things happening and showing up, as opposed to an isolated incident, a pattern may be demonstrated.

In addition to the existence of criminal records or other recorded contacts with the police, which may hinder your ability to obtain employment in the field of criminal justice, activities not rising to the level of an arrest may also become sensitive topics, and possibly disqualifying reasons for hire. Specifically, certain allegations of behavior you may have engaged in or have associations with persons who engage in illegal behaviors, may cause them and you to come to the attention of law enforcement. Many law enforcement agencies that conduct criminal investigations have a system of records, frequently contained in internal databases to assist with analyzing intelligence.

Should you apply for a job with the same agency that may hold adverse intelligence about you—it may hinder your ability to obtain work with that agency. The good news though is that under the Freedom of Information Act, a person who is the subject of a record in a system of records may request access to that record, unless other restrictions may apply (Daniel, 2003). Thus, if you suspect that such information exists, you can request verification and details from that agency.

If you have ever; for example, been on the scene of where an acquaintance was arrested and you were required to supply identification, there is a possibility that such a police contact may be contained in a system of that agency's records. With you strongly considering or already on the path of pursuing a criminal justice career, you might take some time to think about any contacts you have had with the police, and then consider obtaining what information about you that lie within files which may hamper your job prospects. The Privacy Act of 1974 does provide provision for protecting personal privacy by limiting the disclosure of the records it covers; however, remember, law enforcement agencies do share information under certain circumstances.

Once again, police contacts or incident reports can be a source of things that can come back to haunt you. Associates, being in the wrong place at the wrong time – there are any number of investigative agencies that conduct surveillances and if your associations are such that you are hanging around with people who may be engaging in criminal activity, your name, your license plate number, your telephone number; or any number of contacts you had with that person may end up being documented and make their way into any number of intelligence data bases and you may very well not obtain a job and not even know why. Why? How can that happen? Does it matter who one hangs around with in terms of measuring risk? Or do you think recruiters are going to select the person who does not seem to have criminal contacts in their background? So you really need to think about how associations and police contacts may have already affected your prospects for certain jobs.

You have probably heard it said before when you were younger by parents or grandparents that "birds of a feather flock together" or "association breeds assimilation." Yes, it is true that to some extent you can predict what a person will be like based upon the people that they choose to spend their time with. Even though you may have not done anything wrong per se, when agencies are making decisions as to whom to select, some consideration is given to ability to obtain security clearances. Would you back someone you were unsure about? Things that people have done in the past, including associates they spend time with may suggest if they are a good risk. If the shoe were on the other foot, would you choose to hire a person who has evidence of criminal contacts in their background over those who do not?

Juvenile contact with the police, including felony arrests unless you are charged as an adult, usually are exempt from release during background checks. However, if you are still a juvenile you should also avoid detention or arrest as the derogatory information may come out in other ways. For example, there is no prohibition from your friends or family or people you grew up with who know about an incident from providing that information to a background investigator. And recognizing that past behavior is the best predictor of future behavior if an incident rises to a level which would indicate that you present a serious risk to the agency, someone else may get the job.

If your goal is to become a law enforcement officer, there may be any number of other considerations as law enforcement officers are required to carry firearms. As stated, a domestic violence misdemeanor or felony conviction can be reason alone for denying employment in this position. Moreover, a BJS (2003) publication which reported reasons for rejections in firearm's transfers is also revealing. The report included applicant felony convictions (52%); domestic violence misdemeanor conviction or restraining order (14%); and fugitives, mental illness or disability, and drug addiction as rationale for denying gun possession. If one can not obtain a firearm due to unfavorable information coming up in a background check as a civilian, it is not likely that this privilege will be extended to one as a sworn law enforcement officer.

In conclusion, evidence of arrest or conviction is not an automatic disqualification for a criminal justice career. All entries on a criminal record will be factors taken into consideration such as when it happened, under what circumstances, and where you were in your life and when it occurred. Employers will then make assessments, as to how much weight to place on the incident in the decision—making process of hiring you. Most employers will overlook youthful indiscretions if there is no pattern of misconduct spanning throughout your adult life. But again, you have to remember that due to the volume of applications for good jobs, employers are trying to eliminate a certain number of people. It may be enough for certain employers to at least scrutinize your application for other things, or if it comes down to you and another person and all things being equal, the other person without the blemish may get selected. A background investigator logically starts the investigation with a criminal history check so that if there is anything seriously derogatory, a candidate can be disqualified before more time and money is expended in conducting an investigation which has already disclosed enough information to make a decision.

Many records will exist concerning you that will be checked during a background investigation; however, a criminal history record associated with you is something that you do not want to exist at all. A criminal record is regarded negatively by potential employers. It will require a background investigator to expand their efforts, even if it turns out that you were not convicted for the crime you were arrested for. Therefore, it is wise to avoid any negative contact with law enforcement personnel that will result in creation of a criminal record.

Prior work history

Review of your prior work experience can also tell background investigators much about you. A large part of a working person's waking hours is spent each day at work presenting co–workers, and supervisors an opportunity to make assessments about performance and work ethic. Some may also get to know you even more personally. Background investigators capitalize upon these interactions and will likely interview most if not all of your supervisors and a fair share of your co–workers.

Usually background investigators ask general questions of those interviewed permitting them to describe you in whatever fashion they choose. There are usually follow–up questions prepared in the event the responses to the general questions provided do not give a sense of who you are. The background investigator may ask if you have ever been encountered in social settings outside of work and how you behaved then, to include their knowledge of your use or abuse of alcohol. This is designed to assess if you are troublesome in this manner. There are certain expectations employers will have on your new job and if you are viewed as someone who is trouble, there is the possibility that you may not get the job.

Co–workers' and supervisors' responses are very important in determining whether you get a job primarily because it helps the investigator complete a developing composite. Suppose there is some concern that one has a bad temper based upon a criminal record revealing police contact for malicious destruction of property. Moreover several former co–workers indicate that the candidate seems moody much of the time and snaps at others for no good reason. Add to that supervisors indicating that there are client complaints of the candidate demonstrating rage in public contacts. The cumulative effect is that the candidate may have a lowered chance of obtaining the job. Employee interviews alone are not likely to create problems but taken together with other evidence of potential problems can affect decisions on hire. The example of temperament is used here to illustrate the point that no one wants to work with a "hot head" that may be unstable. Any evidence that one exhibits difficulty in controlling anger such as fighting will reflect negatively.

One of the most important questions background investigators will want to know about is the circumstances under which you terminated previous employment. If you terminated your employment for another job paying more money or with more potential or for other valid reasons it will likely be viewed neutrally. However, if you were fired by your employer, a background investigator will seek to determine why. Moreover, there are very few reasons for termination by an employer that is likely to work in your favor other than a lay–off due to budget issues. I do not want to scare you into thinking that because you left a job under less than desirable circumstances that this in an of itself will cause you not to get the job. But if you have been fired from many jobs or left under questionable circumstances it probably will hamper your chances of getting a good CRJ job. You should endeavor to avoid ever getting fired from a job if it is your plan to enter the field of criminal justice.

While at your former work site, the investigator will probably want to take a look at your personnel file. It will be scrutinized for positive and negative references. If the application is in the file, it will be reviewed and compared to any responses given to the prospective employer for consistency. This is why you must be honest in filling out any application or questionnaire—it is the best protection in ensuring that your answers are viewed as consistent versus one who makes it up as he or she goes along. If the personnel file demonstrates that any disciplinary action was taken, it is reflected in the final report and depending upon the circumstances may factor into whether one is hired.

Recently it was reported (Federal Employees News Digest, 2003) that the Internal Revenue Service (IRS) had to revise its internal policies and block access to prohibited internet sites after a 2001 study showed that some IRS employees spent more than half their workday on the internet for personal reasons. And some of these employee's site visits included sexually explicit material and chat rooms. The agency was said to have fired employees who accessed pornography from IRS computers. Conduct such as this contained in a personnel file being reviewed by a background investigator would be viewed as derogatory and highly prejudicial.

A personnel file may also include incidence of complaints brought about by clients, customers, or others with whom one may have interacted. As people sometimes complain without merit, evidence in a personnel file of a criticism alone is not generally enough to affect hiring decisions. However, a pattern of complaints is another matter. I once reviewed a candidate who received rave reviews from most co–workers and supervisors. But there was a substantial number of complaints he had received during encounters with citizens. A pattern existed whereby he was perceived as rude and hostile during his interactions with the public. Only one or two of these allegations were proven to have been founded. However, based upon my review of this information, I was concerned that such a large number of complaints or allegations could be coincidental or merely by chance. This was an atypical situation and in general you should not *worry* about having complaints filed against you, as it is almost inevitable that someone at some time will not see things the way that you do. Thus, as stated a small number of unfounded complaints should not cause any problem; but, if you find yourself receiving a lot of complaints you may want to evaluate the reasons why, so that you may be able to articulate those reasons should it become necessary.

If you are employed in the criminal justice field, it is very important that you are dependable. You are expected at where you are required to be, at the right time, doing what you are charged to do, or there can be consequences. Consider for example, the prosecutor who does not appear in court or the officer who does not make it to a scene on schedule and a dangerous fugitive eludes capture – consequences can be more far-reaching than for other occupations. You must exhibit competency. You need good listening skills to be able to follow instructions and then carry them out. Therefore, the kinds of things that indicate dependability is something prospective employers will want to know when they start to look into your past. So it is very important that no matter what type of job that you have held, that you take into consideration that one day, your current employer may be interviewed and questions posed about your abilities and your willingness to do work assignments and handle them the way they should be carried out.

Needless to say, performance issues such as punctuality, dependability, and productivity are all subject matters for interviews with former bosses and co–workers, as well information sought after in your personnel files. Criminal justice positions require dedicated and hard working people who frequently will not have the benefit of working in the most desirable of environments. Persons who demonstrate that they can not be depended upon or that are lazy are not desirable candidates.

If you were in the military, your position was your job and thus the same questions, concerns and checks will be viewed from the same perspective as any other position. Co–workers will be interviewed. Moreover, your reasons for leaving are likely to be examined. In the military it is a discharging offense to test positive for drugs. Some state or local governments prohibit those having obtained a dishonorable military discharge from obtaining firearms (BJS, 2003) which would limit hiring for sworn law enforcement positions. Being dismissed from any job for drug related reasons is bad news for a career. It can put you in a situation where you may be "black–listed" and thus not likely to gain subsequent employment in the field of criminal justice because oftentimes when you are seeking employment in the field you are expected to list current and past employers—and the reason for leaving those positions. Subsequent to inquire from new employers, past supervisors and co–workers will be interviewed and your person-nel file is reviewed and a determination is made as to whether or not you are viewed as a responsible individual.

References and your reputation

What will "they" say about you? Friends, family, neighbors, landlords, college professors and just about anybody that you can think of may be permitted an opportunity to weigh in on about what they know about you and who they think you are to a background investigator. While your reputation is something that is judged externally, it is something very important to your future. Many criminal justice agencies spend large sums of money for people you have come into contact with in the past to tell about your reputation. But reputation is a funny thing—while you can work to improve it in the future, at the time when critical decisions are made about your future, the questions about your reputation are based on your past actions. I remember during the course of one of the background investigations conducted on me, a colleague told me that she had made some untruthful derogatory statement about me. Then she laughed saying she was joking, adding "are you kidding" as we both knew the reality of the situation was far from what she had told me she said. Character matters. Again, give some thought to what you want others to say about you and act accordingly.

In addition to co–workers and former bosses, a multitude of people you converse with will be contacted and interviewed. Be aware that background investigators are not just going to talk with the people you list as references. Some of these persons will be those you pointed out to the background investigator; however, there will be many who the background investigator will learn about through others and they will be interviewed as well. The expectation is that the people you list as references are going to have pretty good things to say about you. That's why you listed them as references. But to get the full benefit of this piece of the puzzle a background investigator is fashioning, requires talking to more neutral people who see you with less subjective eyes. Also note that people talk and sometimes have a way opening "cans of worms" that others can verify.

Regardless of what "Lulu" or "Johnny–the–rake" is going to say about you, consider what your associates' character will say about you. Whether you know it or not and whether you like it or not, the people you spend time with says something about whom you are. So choose your friends very carefully. I am not referring to appearances or superficial things, but rather things that your friends may have done or even more unfortunately things your friends may drag you into. For example, suppose you have a friend who perpetually does wrong and suppose when interviewed he or she mistakenly attributes some of the illegal activities done with others to you. After all, your friend may be thinking and minimizing that all of his friends do what he does.

A word of caution while we are on the subject: carefully decide who you are willing to endorse by agreeing to become a reference and think about how this may reflect upon you. If it turns out that you recommend people whose character, integrity or performance is questionable it can affect your reputation and your credibility may be diminished.

Reputation of entities you are involved with can also result in perceptions being formed about you. Not only is it difficult for people to separate themselves from their reputation, the same is true of entities. In an article (Campanile, 2001), a university's students and spokesperson weighed in on the Princeton Review Guide's National Student Survey which ranked a university as #1 for "potheads." Although the comments were mixed, the important factor was the Princeton Guide survey's purpose—designed to help parents and students choose schools. There you have it, how many parents want to send their kids off to the "party" college? How many of you could convince your parents that the school that is number one for marijuana users is the best school for you?

I can remember my own efforts to convince my father to permit me to attend my high school. I believe some envy on the part of my father's acquaintance whose child had not been invited to attend this prestigious high school[42] caused her to tell him a rumor of significant drug use at the school. Fortunately, a relative convinced my father to let me attend. Believing her at first, I was still concerned that there was drug use occurring at the school; therefore I became vigilant and cautious. As it turned out, the envious parent was wrong. Not only did I see no evidence of widespread drug use, indeed during my four years at that school, I did not encounter any drug use there.

So there is much that can be determined about you simply based on the reputation of people and entities you have involvement with purely based on inferences. What people actually say about you, especially if there is mounting evidence to support the position is what really counts. Hopefully, there are many people who have positive things to say besides your mother and your best friend. But because this is not a test I have even seen situations where people closest to a candidate provide damaging information. This did not happen as an intention to injure the candidate so much as there was derogatory information to reveal. Consider for example the family member that is one's landlord. The bills must be paid on a property even if it is a relative who is renting, so a failure to pay the rent may result in legal action. Tenant records and interviews with a landlord, whether or not the person is a relative, can reveal evidence of irresponsibility. Other questions for landlords besides if you paid, are if your rent payments were timely, and whether there is outstanding rent. A background investigator will also want to know if monies are still owed to the landlord if you have moved, as well as about any complaints (i.e. loud parties, damage, etc.) against you while you resided there. Because landlords depend upon tenants to pay rent, I have found they are more forthcoming with information to those making inquires – especially if outstanding rents went uncollected. Any records available may be requested for review.

---

[42] My high school invited students to attend who had demonstrated high scholastic achievement.

Concluding remarks

The essence of what a prospective employer is trying to determine is whether you have demonstrated responsible behavior in your past. That certainly is a question posed to previous employers. Were you dependable? Were you trustworthy? Were you responsible? No employer wants to think that when the time comes for you to start work that you are going to be a problem. Again, the best way to predict how you will work in the future is to check out how you worked in the past. If you had a bad boss somewhere—someone who just did not like you or is disgruntled because you left but you did a good job while you were there and you were dependable, it will still come out that way when all information is reviewed. Perhaps there was even one job where you were not as dependable as you should have been maybe due to immaturity, but on other jobs you were dependable. The pattern is what a background investigator is after and the question becomes: does the totality of the circumstances point to responsibility or irresponsibility? Do they point to being a sneaky individual who is untrustworthy or to a person who is honest? What is the overall composite of your life? What does that composite illustrate to someone who views your life from almost every possible angle imaginable?

All of the information background investigators will collect from the many sources checked is compiled and reviewed by a number of people increasingly in rank that will make recommendations about whether to hire you or not. As stated before, getting to this point is a strong indication that an employer is seriously considering hiring you. Thus, at this stage the only thing that can get in your way is your past. Any evidence of derogatory information is viewed from several contexts. Drug use presents a good example of what I mean. It is not just that you have experimented, it is also the context under which it occurred as well – where were you? For example, celebrating your law school graduation by having a few tokes on a marijuana cigarette for the first time (or any time) is probably not a good idea. While it may technically be regarded as experimental use, a situation such as this probably will be viewed more harshly because it is evidence of extremely poor judgment.

Other factors that would be considered in this situation are when it occurred (how long ago), and how it occurred to include who else was there. When one thinks of experimental use, one can imagine a group of people, perhaps partying where one produces a drug and a person never having tried it before is afforded an opportunity to do so. However, when one's actions are more deliberate such as going out and seeking to buy an illegal substance usually does not seem indicative of experimentation. Rather, it lends itself to an interpretation that the person has already tried this drug before and seems willing to spend money and risk freedom by attempting acquisition. Again context is important in determining suitability.

If you believe that you have any issues in your past that may turn up and create problems for you during a background investigation, you should prepare responses ahead of time and be ready to respond. Issues such as gaps in employment or long periods of time when you were not appropriately occupied like being in school may look bad. Be prepared to explain what was going on. Were you able to take care of yourself? Did you walk away from a good job? Were there just things about the job that you did not like? Were you terminated for being viewed as lazy? And know that being paid low wages is not an excuse for being lazy particularly when you consider that criminal justice is definitely one of those lines of work where you will do hard work for relatively low pay. Some have had the attitude that being paid a low wage is a justification for low work effort level. Those with this viewpoint are more than likely to have a problem, as this is the situation for many criminal justice jobs.

The long and short is that your history—every extreme thing that you do or have done potentially may become a subject of a background investigation, may be examined extensively and may become a determining factor in whether or not you get the job that you are seeking.

Chapter 14

Screenings

There are various screenings that you are likely to undergo in your quest for employment in the field of criminal justice. They include: urinalysis screening, polygraph examination, and psychological evaluation. The basis for the various screenings are pretty much the same as with the background investigation in that your prospective employer wants to ensure that you are responsible, dependable, and trustworthy. With respect to truthfulness, these screenings are designed to get right down to the heart of the matter.

The main difference that I note between the two stages of one process is that whereas the background investigation is rather passive, these screenings are right in your face. Consequently, this more intrusive approach to getting to know you may result in some personal discomfort. Also an added element though is that a background investigation to some extent has to do with your willingness to do right by your employer; but the various screenings will go a step further and determine capability. Just because you want to do a good job and are willing to do a good job does not necessarily mean that you are capable of doing a good job. For example, a psychological examination or a physical examination can reveal limitations beyond one's control that would affect ability to do an acceptable job.

Depending upon the agency you opt to work for, you can expect to either have these various screenings conducted in some order simultaneous to your background , or before the background investigation or even after it. Again, it is a good sign to reach the point where these screenings take place in that here too a fair amount of money and time is being invested in assessing if you are likely to work out well for the agency. For every competitive criminal justice position, there are a lot of candidates for the job.

When I applied for the job of police officer in 1977 provides a good example. At that time the Detroit Police Department indicated that for every 100 hundred people who began the process of application, after the various screenings, only 10 people were actually hired. That was decades ago, and today we find even more candidates are likely to apply for a smaller number of jobs making competition very stiff. With sometimes thousands of people applying for a few hundred jobs, employers must have mechanisms whereby they can screen out people to get to that manageable few to consider for selection.

What is important for you to remember is that whether you like it or not, everyone is required to undergo the same process. And so at the screening process, *anything* really can be enough to disqualify you. Apprehension, anger or any negative display of emotion expressed while going through the process is not likely to sit well with a prospective employer and may land you in the category of qualified but not hired. You do not want to go through the weeks and months of the various screening phases only to be told no because there is something in your background that is unacceptable. But also consider the reality that competition is high, and there still exists the possibility that your first choice in positions may escape you, even if you successfully pass all the screenings.

Urinalysis testing for the presence of drugs

I can clearly recall in the mid–eighties my reaction to my employer's decision to test us for the presence of drugs. On one level I felt insulted in that it seemed this was a result that I was not trusted. But on another level, I think it really came down to fear. I knew that I did not use drugs so I was not worried that a test could reveal that I was unless….unless, the test got mixed up or "what if" something was wrong with the test? To make matters worse if indeed there was a problem with the test, how would I defend myself? This over–active imagination caused me to began to develop contingencies in my mind including a plan to submit a specimen to an independent lab immediately after a random sample given at work since that would be the only way I could defend myself against a false positive result as a negative test in the future is no way to prove you were negative at the time the test was administered.

I share my experience with you so you can see that it is natural (I think) for most people to be anxious about an intrusion such as this into their lives. Now over fifteen years later, I rarely give this procedure a second thought. I think what helped me to accept something new, aside from the fact that my fears were never realized[43] was that my agency's objective was to demonstrate to the public that we took being "drug free" to such an extent that we were willing to submit to the testing as a sign of our commitment. I hope that you too can come to terms with the need for drug testing and I will provide suggestions to help you do so.

The first piece of advice I can offer is for you to try not to think of the urinalysis screening as insulting to you. To do this, it is helpful to acknowledge that regardless, of how each of us feels about urinalysis testing for drugs related to work, most of us would agree that criminal justice professionals should be drug–free. Criminal justice professionals are charged with legislating, carrying out, enforcing and prosecuting various illegal acts. We administer the criminal justice system. Such responsibility demands no compromise for engaging in criminal behavior to include obtaining and consuming illegal substances. Moreover, sobriety is necessary in discharging the very important duties of the office we are entrusted to hold.

With such important and pivotal responsibilities, employee drug use could have serious adverse consequences beyond those typically associated with use. When people use drugs they are involved in an altered state of reality. In

---

[43] And no I never did get an independent test. I know I started to feel better when the procedures included sealing your own specimen and that there were two vials—one which would be available for re–test and that you could verify which vial was yours in the event of a problem.

other words, they may be "high" while discharging their duties. Employers are concerned about safety issues as well when drug use is an issue. Oftentimes public servants must operate vehicles or other types of machinery—some carry weapons and may exercise deadly force if the situation calls for it. The judgment of criminal justice professionals should not be clouded by mind altering substances.

Employees using drugs could result in a situation where drug evidence is stolen and consumed or resold on the illegal drug market. Such employees may engage in any host of crimes that serious drug abusers commit, such as stealing from co–workers. And then there is the potential to taint the very investigations the individuals may be involved in. For example, usually when you hear about these cases where employees have been involved in stealing drug evidence, prosecutors examine all of the pending cases that this person was working. The result is frequently prosecutors' global declination to prosecute pending cases—even closed cases may be re–opened. The reason for this is that the prosecutor knows that these situations will be exploited by defense attorneys and the credibility of the CRJ professional is now highly questionable. The defense attorney will try to exploit the fact that this criminal justice practitioner has severe human frailties which may have affected their decision–making in that particular case. So with that in mind, I hope I have given a pretty good rationale for why it is that criminal justice agency administrators feel the need to ensure that their workforce is free from drug use.

Having established the importance of CRJ professionals remaining drug–free, the second piece of advice I can offer to help you mentally deal with the fact that you will have to submit to urinalysis screening is that if you do not use drugs, the test is not really administered for you. Unfortunately, everyone is not truthful about their drug use, and it is for these few that the test is needed. I am as much of an idealist as the next person wanting to believe in my fellow CRJ professionals, but all it takes is one example to shatter idealism. I am aware of a former CRJ professional who had been on her job for probably 25 years or more when she ended up testing positive for marijuana use and she lost her job. It was a lose–lose situation. She suffered the stigma, and embarrassment associated with a public hearing about the situation and her employer had to take adverse action against a tenured employee. You see, one positive drug test result of an employee is evidence that everyone will not be truthful in demonstrating a commitment to remain drug–free. So there is a need for the test, but try not to take it personal if you do not use drugs.

Drug use is a hot topic in American culture these days and debated regularly and rigorously. There are some that would move to have drugs legalized. One thing I have noticed though is that those who would favor drug legalization usually do not emanate from the CRJ community. Criminal justice professionals in general would be expected to either remain neutral on such issues or at least to maintain the status quo of existing laws that answer the question of whether a given behavior is viewed as right or wrong based on its legality or illegality. However, there are public figures who have taken a contrary position on this issue. For example Governor Gary Johnson (New Mexico) came under fire for his ideology and move to try and legalize drugs and his disclosure of having used marijuana and cocaine (CNN, 1999). Regardless of one's position on drug legalization, there are those who would rationalize that if a politician can use drugs, why can't they?

What I want you to take note of is that most positions in the field of criminal justice are not the result of political selections[44] which would present them with wider latitude in the things appointees may say or do. Conversely, most public servant CRJ positions are governed by standards of conduct which to a certain extent puts you in a position where you are held to a higher standard than even politicians in that your disclosure or your having engaged in certain types of behavior, such as drug use can disqualify you from

---

[44] There are some people that while considered as CRJ professions, the origins of their appointment originates from an election or appointment by a government head (i.e. President, Governor, etc.). Examples of such positions would be County Sheriffs and federal agency heads.

certain jobs. Even policy makers responsible for allowing urinalysis screening within federal law enforcement agencies and encouraging these screenings within in the workplace, are not necessarily subjected to this testing which is illustrative of the fact the standards of political office are not the same thing as that of CRJ positions. Bad acts on the part of political figures are frequently judged by constituents who fire them, but government employees usually can be dismissed for much less. Your focus should be on the fact that use of illicit drugs remains illegal in this country and commit yourself to the challenge of remaining drug free and willing to prove that you are so on demand.

In addition to those who may lie about drug use, there are also those who may try and beat the drug test. These attempts range from drinking herbal teas to "clean" their body systems to putting certain chemicals into the specimens themselves to having others provide the sample; people have tried to cheat on urinalysis tests almost from the inception of their use. Discussion of this issue is not initiated to give one advice on how to beat a test, but rather to dissuade one from trying to beat the drug test. I have proclaimed throughout this entire book, if you have serious issues such as drug abuse, the best thing for you to do is to avoid seeking employment in the criminal justice field as opposed to trying to figure out ways of concealing the existence of these problems. There really is no reason to try and beat the drug test because there is only a small chance that one will succeed. Any attempt to tamper with a urine specimen is not likely to work, but also in detection which will result in sudden disqualification for candidates seeking CRJ employment. Moreover, even users of drugs who abstain for a period[45] to legitimately pass the drug test have no good reason needlessly putting themselves in this situation as even if they are not caught in the initial screening, there are other safeguards in place to catch them as well. One could

---

[45] This might not work anyway as different drugs remain in one's system for varying periods of time. Believe it or not, marijuana is detectable in one's system substantially longer than cocaine and heroin.

get the job and then undergo a random check which could result in losing the job down the line.

I have discussed reasons for avoiding drug use at length in this book, but what if you have already used drugs before? How much is too much? Is there a magic number that will result in automatic disqualification for many CRJ positions? Perhaps this discussion is most easily broached by identifying what constitutes a serious drug problem for purposes of working in the field of criminal justice. Persons who have been diagnosed as addicted[46] to a particular drug probably will experience difficulty in obtaining employment in the field of criminal justice or if they do, they may experience trouble with carrying out the duties of their positions. For example, substantial drug use or use of certain drugs can result in brain damage that may even affect the psychological test results. Some state or local governments also reject persons from obtaining firearms if they are drug addicted (BJS, 2003). Sustained drug use over time can lead to a "burned–out" appearance and mental impairment to the point that judgment may be noticeably affected prior even to hire.

There are many agencies that will not consider hiring a person who has experimented with certain drugs. Drugs with a high potential for addiction, brain damage or violence are among those CRJ administrators are most concerned about. The fact that many of the offenders that end up circulating through the criminal justice system have been abusers of drugs presents these administrators with first hand experience of the fall–out involved with those who have chosen to seriously abuse drugs. For the most part, a person who has used any illicit drug besides mari-

---

[46] Even persons not in the field of criminal justice found to have been addicted may have problems with retaining positions. Recently the U.S. Supreme Court ruled that an employer can refuse to rehire a drug addict in recovery as long as its policy is neutral and applies to all workers, not just addicts in recovery. The court upheld the position of Raytheon Co, which had refused to rehire a worker who had been forced to resign two years earlier after a positive drug test (Drug Enforcement Report, 2003).

juana may experience difficulty in obtaining employment in the criminal justice system. A good exercise would be for you think about various drugs and what you know about them and how people act when they are under the influence of these drugs. Now ask yourself if you would feel comfortable with someone under the influence of that drug while discharging the duties of an important CRJ position. To get a feel for what others think from different walks of life, especially conservative thinkers, broach the topic with others.

Some agencies[47] have provided guidelines to their recruitment staff about standards for disqualification of candidates which may have numbers attached to them. However, this information is held "close to the vest". Moreover, for me to reveal what I personally know about these numbers would be unethical. But I believe most of us know intuitively how many times a person can use drugs before it is regarded as more than merely experimental. I believe that if you think about it or discuss it with others, you could come up with a reasonable number that one could use to identify anything beyond which would not be considered experimental use. Again, keep in mind that among law enforcement executives rests some of the most conservative thinkers around. In thinking about this, if you have ever used drugs you should consider how you line up with the norm you determine from your studies. Would your past drug use be regarded as experimental; recreational; or addiction level? You need to address this issue as I daresay, some readers may have already crossed the line. If one's drug use falls into any category besides experimental, it may be difficult if not impossible to obtain work in the field of CRJ after graduation. Some may need to face the possibility of not being able to pursue a job they have wanted up to this point.

There have been those who have felt that who they know can guarantee them hire regardless of where they have

---

[47] The U.S. Drug Enforcement Administration recently amended its job announcements to include identification of the drugs which will disqualify a candidate previously using the named drugs.

stood on the drug issue. However, who you know may be able to help you, but there are still minimum screening qualifications which must be met which may not be waived absent the concurrence of many high ranking people. Might I suggest for those who know someone in an agency that has been a mentor, that this subject is broached to help you determine if you can qualify for a position. Those who seek having exceptions made for them not only subject themselves to embarrassment but also the person who is vouching for them although as a practical matter a mentor will not find out about a candidate's drug abuse from the agency due to privacy issues. There have been times even when a CRJ practitioner parent wishes a child to follow in their footsteps and the offspring is not hired—in some of those cases it has been because the children of CRJ professionals have engaged in bad behavior unbeknownst to the parent.

On the issue of drug experimentation, it is not just how many times one has used a particular drug that will likely be an issue, but as already stated at what point in one's life it occurred. It is as they say "timing is everything." Drug experimentation occurring while in high school or middle school, will likely be viewed very differently than if it happened in your junior year of college as a criminal justice major. You can certainly understand how a criminal justice administrator may view the timing of your decision to experiment as a factor, since a decision to experiment with drugs bears on your judgment ability.

Even the circumstances of experimentation may become an issue. For example, consider the following scenario: Lets say there is Bob, an individual in a party setting where a marijuana joint is being passed around the room takes one puff off the joint whether or not he inhales, and then stops. In comparison, like Bob, Bill is at a party where a joint is being passed once and he takes a hit, then the joint is passed again, he takes another hit. The party moves to another location, more marijuana is produced and Bill takes hits all night long and then the next day the crew gets together again and there is more of the same. Both Bill and Bob claim to never have experimented with marijuana again. Certainly you have experimentation in both of these exam-

ples presented, but as you can see the volume of experimentation of Bob may have resulted in a "buzz" versus Bill who
was likely to have gotten "stoned." If I am the deciding official in this case, Bill, especially if there is anything else derogatory in his background is going to have a problem
getting the job.

In conclusion, the purpose for a urinalysis screening test
is to make sure that people who are currently using drugs
are detected and denied employment. Having used drugs at
any point in your life is likely to be a sensitive subject for
you as the question is likely to be asked[48] in addition to any
urine sample you must provide. Thus, the best advice I can
give you is IF YOU HAVE NEVER USED DRUGS, FOR
THE SAKE OF YOU FUTURE CAREER, IF YOU ARE A
CRIMINAL JUSTICE MAJOR, PLEASE DO NOT START
NOW!

The polygraph exam

I would venture to bet that if I asked candidates about
which part of the CRJ screening process they are most
frightened about, it would be the polygraph examination
hands down. Those taking a polygraph exam may feel even
more uncomfortable than submitting to a urinalysis
screening. Perhaps you have never thought of submitting to
a polygraph exam and have difficulty believing its reputation to scare people. Well consider for example that when
some law enforcement recruiters mention during orienta-
tions that a polygraph examination is required, the pool of
candidates immediately shrinks. I recently learned from
one executive who monitors and enforces police standards

---

[48] For example, the U.S. Drug Enforcement Administration includes a Drug Questionnaire on websites associated with vacancy
announcements for positions. The questionnaire is very intrusive
and requires applicants to disclose the types of substances they
have tried and when they were tried. Moreover, candidates must
certify that their answers are truthful and the form asserts that
"misstatement of fact or omission of information" may subject the
candidate to disqualification for further consideration in the hiring process.

in his state that it is not unusual to begin a law enforcement orientation session for new applicants with 500 individuals; however, after advising the candidates about the statewide requirement of a polygraph exam—only about 150 individuals return after a break.

Not every criminal justice employer uses polygraph exams for screening applicants;[49] however, I believe the trend is for more and more of them to do so. So you should expect that before long many of them will learn of its benefits for screening and prepare accordingly. If you will be subjected to a polygraph for a position, it should not come as a surprise to you among the strict standards is your right to a written notice before testing (Department of Labor, 1988). You should also be mindful that in addition to the polygraph being used as a screening device for employment, as is the case for drug testing, polygraph tests are administered in some CRJ agencies for certain positions throughout a career either routinely or for a specific purpose. The Energy Department recently proposed a rule to polygraph employees as a means to root out spies (Federal Employees Digest, 2003). Remember, the more highly desirable the position is, the more likely that there will be more screenings involved such as the polygraph exam. Although to be expected, I know that this is not reassuring as many are nervous about undergoing a polygraph exam.

Those expecting to undergo a polygraph exam are probably frightened on many levels. There are a lot of things that come into your mind when you are faced with a procedure that has such a range of connotations associated with it. It is just natural that we do not want to be examined rigorously in the form of a dissection. One may feel like he or she is under a microscope. There is something that just rises up in us—a level of indignation with just the thought of knowing that you are going to be hooked up to a machine, wires

---

[49] In fact the Employee Polygraph Protection Act prohibits most private employers from using the lie detector tests either for pre–employment or during the course of employment. However, federal, state and local governments are not affected by the law (U.S. Department of Labor, 1988).

are going to be connected to you and questions—I might add uncomfortable questions are going to be asked of you. And just the very nature of the fact that you have to undergo this process is enough to make you feel uncomfortable.

The very word polygraph is enough to cause most of us some discomfort especially at the thought that the word is used in the same sentence as our own names. No you are not crazy for feeling this way. Without any intention whatsoever to deceive, thoughts immediately are conjured up about whether one can trust a machine, not to mention the examiner to do right by you. And then there are the concerns about whether the polygraph machine or interpreter of results will really pick up the truth that you know you are telling. There is the fear of really being truthful and the machine indicates otherwise. You may feel that you know what your intentions are, but what if this second party who has a machine hooked up to you picks up on something that is not real.

Moreover, no matter what they tell you, there is always tucked away the concern that they might ask about that one thing you never wanted anyone to know about. Let's face it, although not germane to what the examiner may be seeking, we all have got things floating around in our head that we just want to have left there undisturbed. It could be that you have something that you do not want disclosed that may have nothing whatsoever to do with the CRJ position you may be seeking which can also contribute to a level of discomfort. Focusing in on the purpose of the exam may help with alleviating anxiety, especially if it is your intention to tell the truth and if you do not have anything relevant to hide.

The primary purpose of the polygraph exam is to ascertain if the things that you have included in your previous written and oral statements accurately represents what is really going on in your life. You may find it hard to believe, but there are people who are not always truthful in admitting that there are things that they have done. A hint about what will be asked is to review your application and other related documents for sensitive topics such as drug use, or past criminal behavior. In effect, the main purpose for the polygraph is just to ensure that you are sincere about the things that you have already disclosed. If you can regard the polygraph exam as confirming everything you have already stated, this stage of the process may be easier for you to stomach.

From the same philosophical standpoint as with urinalysis screening, if you have been truthful in the responses given, the polygraph examination was not designed for you. The whole point in administering a polygraph exam as an employment tool is to root out people who are untruthful. And as is the case with the drug testing, since agencies do not know up front who is truthful, if this is a screening mechanism utilized by an agency, it must be administered to each candidate. Because your new employer does not yet know you as well as perhaps your friends do, they have to check everyone. And even if they know you, consistency requires that if the agency chooses to employ a screening technique, to be fairly administered requires that all candidates must be subjected to it. It would be discriminatory to check some people and not other people. So if a test is administered, they would have to test everyone. You can not wiggle out of it regardless of who are or who you happen to know.

What if anything can one do to clam down in anticipation of taking a polygraph exam? My best advice in terms of easing your mind in respect to the polygraph is simply this: If you are a person who is being truthful and who is not trying to misrepresent facts on your application, the polygraph exam should prove simply an exercise presenting you with an opportunity for you to demonstrate that you can handle uncomfortable situations. Think of the polygraph exam in the same manner as you would the metal detector and other screening devices at an airport security checkpoint. Prior to the terrorist attacks on September 11, 2001, many people just saw the whole thing as a nuisance. It was difficult to see the need. However, after terrorists were able to slip through security with weapons used to carry out their attacks, we now see the need for effective screenings. One now can better see that the metal detectors in the airport are not for those who do not have any weapons or prohibited items, it is for detection of the people who are trying to sneak on the airplane that have something dangerous they are trying to conceal. It is designed to identify those persons so they can be weeded out.

Similarly, it is the same thing with the polygraph in that the purpose is to expose those who wish to conceal material information relevant to decision–making concerning hire. I do not know if this polygraph–metal detector analogy is enough to get you to feel like you want to run out and get a lie–detector test tomorrow. But I hope it helps you to know that if you do not intend to lie, then no one will be trying to catch you in a lie. If you think of it in terms of that is the reason, then you can logically conclude that no one is accusing you of anything; no one believes that you are an untrustworthy person. It is simply a screening device and just another phase that you have to go through. And again, it is not for those intent on telling the truth. Endeavor to be truthful in your responses.

Besides a commitment to tell the truth, remembering that the polygraph test is not designed to catch you in a lie unless you intend to tell one, knowing that the test is being administered by another human should also help ease your nerves. They are people just like you. Moreover, since your test is not likely to be the first that they have ever administered, probably any nervousness on your part will be regarded as just that—nerves. Polygraphists are trained to detect deception and so if it is not your intent to deceive, again you should not have a problem. In my interactions with polygraph operators I have concluded that as a group they do not appear as people who are out to get anyone. I view them as professionals who objectively use their skills to determine the truth regardless of which side the truth is most favorable to. However, I also view them as shrewd enough that if one intentionally intends to deceive, the polygraph operator will detect this.

I have also heard the stories about people trying to beat the polygraph examination. Some believe if they act a certain way, if they are overly calm, if they breathe a certain way, if they say things a certain way—that these things will help them fool the machine and manipulate the results of the test. There exists substantial dialogue available on the internet concerning how to beat a polygraph test. The advice of some warns potential applicants that as long as they do not admit to anything when taking a polygraph that they do not have to worry about being denied a job. It is when they admit to being untruthful is when they are in danger of not getting the job.

Still other chat entries over the internet are from persons desperate to learn how to beat the polygraph examination because they have something in their pasts to hide, such as drug use. Clearly, these persons regret decisions they have made, but there is nothing they can do to erase the past. You on the other hand with your future before you can endeavor to avoid behavior you may regret and worry about having to disclose. Concentrating on how to beat the polygraph is not the answer. Your surest way for passing the polygraph is to tell the truth. The real story is always out there. Even if one lies, as suggested and never admits to the lie, does not necessarily guarantee hire.

A good investigator will discover the truth by checking into the various clues available. For example, if you are untruthful and you do not fess up to it, there are agencies, because of the nature of their mission and operation that still will not hire you. Moreover there are other ways of determining or substantiating whether the truth is being told besides the polygraph. The polygraph exam may show only an indication of deception, but if deception is really at issue, there may be documents which can be reviewed, people that can be interviewed or any number of things out there that can point to the truth. And the problem that you may face in addition to not getting the job if you lie on an application or misrepresent the facts may occur in future application of other jobs when inconsistencies are detected.

Oftentimes in positions of criminal justice if you apply for a position with another agency, that new agency will inquire if you have ever applied for a job in this field before and request identification of the agencies involved. It is not

beyond the realm of possibility, especially if there is a concern about untruthfulness that the new prospective employer will confer with other agencies' applications to see if
you were consistent in your responses given. If one is
caught in a lie this way, not only is there the risk of not getting the job, but one could be put in a position to be
"black–listed." As bad as the truth may seem, even if it is a
situation that may preclude you from getting the job you
want you still do not want to get into telling falsehoods or
misrepresenting the facts because you can run into even
more problems.

The situation of telling a lie and the truth coming out
later is so problematic that it can lead to not only affecting a
job prospect, but if you are already in a sensitive criminal
justice position, it may affect your current job. I am aware of
a situation where an individual attempted to upgrade to a
better position within the same criminal justice agency. For
the current job, the person did not have to submit to a polygraph examination, but for the second job it was a requirement. After being selected under a competitive process, this
person failed the polygraph and later admitted to giving
conflicting statements about drug experimentation upon
initial hire versus during the background process for the
new more sensitive position. Consequently, the offer for the
new job was withdrawn. Moreover, the stigma associated
with this experience remains. In a situation where the
truth is uncovered by background investigators having to
pull it out of you or some other source, it will likely be factored unfavorably into decision–making for hire. And for
the really wonderful jobs where there is substantial competition, being caught in a lie will likely result in one being
eliminated from the process.

A way to mentally prepare for the polygraph examination is to try and anticipate which questions will be asked of
you. Another body of information available on the internet
is vendors that provide practice tests for those anticipating
a polygraph exam. While I do not agree with any effort to assist anyone with concealing deception, I do believe that the
more one can prepare oneself in the form of identifying
what to expect is ethical and can be helpful. For example,

University Student Criminal Justice Clubs may consider inviting polygraph examiners and other professionals, such as psychologists to speak about what candidates may expect as they proceed through the various screening processes.

As stated, since the purpose of the polygraph is to substantiate what you have already stated, you can anticipate which questions will be asked by reviewing documents you have already submitted. Moreover, although not as reassuring, you have to expect that any question that you answered in preparation for your background investigation in any area of your life, no matter how embarrassing, which would reflect upon your integrity for the position for which you are applying may be a topic broached during the polygraph examination. And because, my approach is to get you prepared for what to expect, you should also anticipate that the most embarrassing thing you have ever done may be a question posed to you. If that most embarrassing experience is not criminal, or unethical you should be okay. You should be prepared to truthfully answer that question when posed or face the range of consequences described. Just getting past the most embarrassing thing ever, probably will result in a more relaxed demeanor when you show up and help you precede positively through one of the most uncomfortable aspects of the process to selection for the job of your dreams!

In conclusion, the key to getting through the stress of having to undergo a polygraph exam is not to believe your employer thinks *you* are a liar. But rather, its administration to every candidate, including you, is to detect and screen out for hire candidates that have lied about their background. Start preparing for the polygraph examination before you are actively seeking employment. Do not wait to finally look down the road to determine if you can make it through the various screenings to include what could become for you the "dreaded" polygraph exam. As has been demonstrated throughout this book, the background investigation and screenings such as the polygraph exam are efforts of your prospective employer to check deep into your past. There is only one way you can avoid the embarrassment of answering questions you do not want to and that is by not applying for certain jobs, especially when you know what will be required of you. If one's background is so sullied that passing a background check is impossible, why put yourself through it all?

Psychological exams

About all I can say on this topic is that there may be a psychological examination administered for some CRJ positions. If the psychologists are the professionals they are touted to be, there should be nothing one can do to prepare for a psychological examination. One is either sane or not. Either one has emotional or mental problems he or she is coping with effectively to work in a sensitive criminal justice position or not. Most of the positions I am aware that require a psychological examination, written or oral, are law enforcement positions where one is given substantial authority including the use of deadly force since firearms are carried. Mental illness or disability in a person is also a reason to legally prohibit the transfer of a firearm (BJS, 2003) which would limit capability of obtaining a law enforcement job. The main thing is just that a psychologist will want to make sure that one is not "crazy" or that views held are not so radically off–key or incongruent with the ideology or the mission of the agency for which one is seeking employment that it would be disruptive.

Interviews

Interviews can be as much of a screening mechanism as any other part of the process. For our purposes, I just want to reiterate the importance of being truthful in your responses as the consistency of what you say during your interview will be checked out in other stages of the process. Recognizing that most of the screenings are expensive endeavors, do not be surprised if interviewers ask some of the tough questions up front as doing so permits them an opportunity to screen out undesirable candidates as quickly as possible so they can concentrate on expending funds on the more competitive and qualified candidates. Remember it is worse to be caught in a lie than it is to reveal something uncomfortable or embarrassing. Some agencies may already have the answers to questions posed. Moreover, knowing the reasons why you are seeking the particular position of public service can pay off here. One key to arriving at a decent response is knowing what you are getting yourself into; in other words knowing the job.

The DOs

Although my experience with sports has been very limited I note that offense appears to be a superior position as opposed to defense. Consequently, oftentimes when I am working through a particular issue I choose the offense posture. I believe this approach can also be helpful in getting ahead of the curve to prepare for a background check to enter the field of criminal justice. In addition to the information contained in other parts of this book, this section provides some positive practical suggestions that can help you on a proactive basis to make it through a background investigation favorably.

This book provides an opportunity for you to identify how criminal justice managers, in particular law enforcement managers, think. In other words, what types of things do they take into consideration when they are making decisions about one of the most important things that happens in your life—the beginning of your career. Much of what has been discussed about background investigation and screenings are the types of things that can cause you woe. This section provides examples of some things that can work out on the plus side. In particular, what kinds of things can you do to demonstrate that you are a responsible person?

As stated, exhibiting responsible behavior is likely to be viewed favorably by a prospective CRJ employer. You have an opportunity to demonstrate responsible behavior in your regular interactions, such as in your current job, and in interpersonal relationships. But in terms of the extra–credit, what kinds of things can you do that can be beneficial? First of all, community service should never be underplayed. It is something that permits a look into a person in that it demonstrates a willingness to go beyond what is normally expected. It indicates that one is willing to give of something very precious, namely time, and without seeking monetary compensation.

I am not referring to a job that may involve social work, where one receives some type of compensation, which is noble, but very different from mentoring kids or teens in need without payment. Or involvement in a program where you are feeding the homeless—or any number of gestures conducted on a voluntary basis. Community service as viewed by some employers is a sign of more than responsibility because you demonstrate that you are willing to do something above and beyond without expecting to receive credit. I am not suggesting that you engage in volunteer work solely as a means by which you can ingratiate future employers to get a job. Usually people who engage in volunteer work do so from the heart, and if you are not doing it because you want to or out of other gratuitous motives, it will become obvious anyway. However, if you *are* inclined to volunteer and give of yourself, it is certainly likely to be looked upon favorably by potential CRJ employers. If you are or have engaged in volunteer work in the past, drop the modesty and ensure that you include this information in your resume to assist your prospective employer in getting to know you better. Working as a volunteer also permits you to pick up skills that can be useful to you in your career in criminal justice. These may be skills that you may not have the opportunity to acquire any other way.

Second, another thing that you can do that can add value to your background is to work as hard as you possibly can on your current job and to do a very good job. Avoid being lazy and overly causal about your job. If you give an honest day's work for an honest day's pay, then you are likely to come out okay. It is wrong to accept pay if you are not willing to do the work expected of you. It will come across if one is unwilling to work. And hopefully your hard, skillful, productive work will be rewarded. Awards, accolades and other recognition look impressive on applications and resumes. Moreover, if you do a really good job and are helpful at work, your co—

workers and your supervisors will hopefully have wonderful things to say about you which should also ensure that
there are beneficial aspects of your past that will show
through during the course of any investigation of your background.

Third, another proactive thing that you can do is to avoid
"short–cuts." I have noticed that persons who try to take the
short way or seek to make a quick buck have problems because details are important. Do not ignore the details, especially in a field where if details are ignored or overlooked,
justice may not be served. Try and avoid short cuts as one
draw back to cutting corners is your productivity at work
can suffer resulting in poor evaluations. Being efficient is
expected but not at the expense of over–looking key considerations.

Fourth, avoid all drug use, all drug experimentation. If
you have read this book, and you have never experimented
with drugs in your life – please do not start now. Do not
start while you are in college pursuing a degree in criminal
justice or a law program—this is not the time to experiment. If you have never done drugs, commend yourself and
vow never to succumb to this temptation whether it be
based on peer pressure, curiosity or anything else that
would make you try drugs. Anyone who has ever abused or
used drugs that would speak honestly to you would say that
the drugs never did anything good for them. Therefore,
there is no reason to try drugs out, because everything that
is around the corner after trying them is negative. Even if
you decided to experiment, especially if it is recent relative
to when you apply, it can affect your ability to get certain
jobs.

Fifth, be a professional while discharging your duties.
You want to be remembered as someone who is competent
while polite. In essence, "do your job!" If you do your job
well, even if a boss cannot remember specifics, when your
past performance is being checked on your previous job(s),
supervisors and co–workers will hopefully have positive
things to say about you, but surely nothing derogatory
should come to mind. And even if there is one person who

makes negative statements relative to you, if the over–whelming responses are positive, your background evaluator may discount the extremist as someone with an "ax to grind" or perhaps as an isolated situation. So there is no reason not to do the right thing by not doing your job. It will only benefit you. To do the opposite is going to hurt you in the long run.

Sixth, "don't complain, don't explain." If you do something wrong, take the hit. It may come out later anyway. Meanwhile, your conscience will be eased. In the short–term the consequences may not be that pleasant; however in the long–run it is going to be viewed much better. We all make mistakes, and so the best thing to do in those instances where mistakes are made is to take constructive criticism, learn and endeavor to do better in the future.

Seventh, promote a state of being "easy going;" avoid temper tantrums. If you are a person who angers easily, you may want to avoid this particular field, but certainly any outbursts of anger, anything that would give a new employer reason to think that you will "go postal" at the drop of a hat will likely hamper your chances of getting into the field of criminal justice. Or if you are already in the field, maintaining your employment could be jeopardized by outbursts of anger. Usually if one is out–of–control and does not maintain self–control, the consequences of what can happen tend to be steep. So keep your temper in check, especially when you are at work.

Eight, go light on the booze. Yes alcoholic beverages tend to be relaxing, but they can lower your inhibitions to such an extent that you may do things or say things that you may feel silly about later on. You might also engage in behavior that will minimize your likelihood of getting a position in the field of criminal justice. How much alcohol you regularly consume as well as how you behave when you do partake may become an issue during any examination of your background.

I realize that some people reading this book will debate my opinions; however, what is written in this book is real from the perspective of a criminal justice professional. I expect some to even assert that certain aspects of the process of becoming a CRJ professional are not "fair." And you may even have a point to argue, but what is the advantage of taking a position that inevitably may result in not obtaining the job you want? Having to undergo an overwhelming level of scrutiny may not seem fair in the whole scheme of things, but the reality of the situation is that this is just the way things are.

You can choose to debate the merits or the fairness of the ideology of those who will determine your fate with respect to obtaining positions in the field—or you can come to grips with the motivation and determination of CRJ agencies' commitment to hiring the most suitable persons available which necessitates much of the practices associated with background investigation. Armed with this information you can face this reality and go on to determine how you can conform or otherwise make changes in your life to ensure that when the time comes for you to try and get one of these great jobs that you will be in a position to do so.

Another possibility is that some will make an assessment and determine that there are things in their lives they are unwilling to give up. Are there parts of your personal life that you are unwilling to have opened up to others? Not just when you are seeking employment with an employer looking backwards, but looking into your life while you are working as a criminal justice professional, and then to the future. Only you can answer these questions.

I hope that there is much discussion generated as a result of this book. Because this part focused primarily on what to expect of the hiring process for highly desirable CRJ positions, Life Application Exercises were not included. However, I do believe some benefit may be derived from your thinking about and discussing the concept of background investigations. I believe it can be helpful in your buying into the concept of these necessary intrusions, as well as, a review in determining how well you have grasped the concepts introduced. Therefore, give some thought to and discussion to the following:

1) If you were a criminal justice professional, what would be some of the things that you would take into consideration when conducting background investigations?

2) Why do you suppose that background investigations are conducted? Why would the specific criminal justice agency you are most considering working for determine a need to engage in background checks?

3) Do you believe that urinalysis screening for the presence of drugs and polygraph examinations are necessary procedures? Why or why not are they necessary?

Concluding comments

As unpleasant as background investigations may seem to candidates planning to work in the field of criminal justice, hopefully this section has demonstrated that they exist and are not likely to cease. Employers consider background investigations as necessary because they do not know you. You are a complete stranger to them usually when you walk into their door. And we all know how society reacts to strangers. We are somewhat apprehensive of them, and to a large extent it is the responsibility of the ominous stranger to set our minds at ease and demonstrate that he or she can be trusted; hence, the need for background investigations.

The overwhelming guiding question is can this individual be trusted? Is he or she someone agency secrets can be entrusted to? Can it be reasonably assured that confidential information is expected to remain confidential in the hands of this person? Will this person be dependable and come to work on time? Is this individual responsible and will he or she do the job very well? In short, who is this person seeking to come into our closed community? We have to protect ourselves. Most organizations have their own culture[50] and I would suggest strongly that you try to learn as much as possible about the agencies that you are seeking employment with prior to submitting application for hire. This will not only help you in interviews but also help to lessen a major culture shock when you walk into the door. Nonetheless, all of these are things that your employer is likely to take into consideration when they begin to check out your past. Not only are the aforementioned factors overwhelming reasons for conducting a background investigation, but the fact that the process can be used to streamline the number of eligible people is also a benefit to CRJ employers.

There are so many criminal justice majors[51] and a finite number of criminal justice positions making the field very competitive with some particularly desirable jobs even more so than others. For competitive positions with many applicants, employers try to eliminate some of the numbers. Let us consider an example of a given CRJ employer intending to hire 100 people for which 10,000 applications have been received. In effect, this employer would have to rule out 9,900 people so they can get to the 100 people they are going to hire. There are several screening mechanisms which may be employed. Some jobs will have a physical requirement; still other jobs require certain licenses, such as a driver's license or state certification. Some of the people applying will not meet minimum requirements; so lets say that's half in our example and the agency gets the number down to 5,000. Okay, so how do they whittle the number down more? Recall, that one technique is to identify as early as possible people who will not pass a background investigation anyway, before any funds or additional time are expended in this regard. What about looking at things like credit? Some agencies will ask certain questions up front even during an interview before a conditional offer is made.

---

[50] Even within the field of criminal justice, different organizations have different cultures. This is never more evident on a macro level than when agencies merge (if you do not believe me ask any employee currently working within the newly formed Department of Homeland Security) or on the micro level when employees transfer to different agencies.

[51]Moreover, criminal justice agencies do not generally limit hire to only criminal justice majors.

If there is a serious problem, such a person could be eliminated early in the process, all in an effort to get the applicant pool down to a manageable level while still giving everyone equal opportunity. So getting to know who you are while simultaneously identifying the most competitive candidates is a vantage point from which agencies operate. What about you? From what position should you regard the whole process?

As a prospective candidate for a professional position in the criminal justice field, you should endeavor to learn as much as possible about the background requirements for the positions you expect to apply for. Heaven forbid, and it has happened to people, that you would spend all of this time, money and other resources, really get your mind set on a job and yet because there is a background requirement you cannot meet, it is unlikely that you will get the job. It is most important that you are realistic in your assessments. If one will be substantially hampered by his or her past that getting the job is unlikely, it is probably better to decide as early as possible whether a change in major or career direction is in order. People who determine that their background is problematic to achieving the goal of working in the criminal justice field, if hired may also experience future problems.

In the field of criminal justice, it is not just past behavior of employees that comes under scrutiny. For one's entire career, much of what you do will be studied and judged. And if you are someone who likes to just live your life without being concerned about how your actions will be viewed by others, or if not concerned about scrutiny but you do a lot of things that perhaps fall in the gray area, reconsider whether the criminal justice field is for you. There are certainly careers out where one can engage in shady practices and not be concerned about losing one's job. But in the criminal justice field, not only is it a possibility, it is almost a certainty that if you are detected to be involved in criminal behavior you will be terminated. In fact, you do not even have to be convicted of a crime to lose your job in criminal justice, because frequently, the standards of conduct for these types of positions, forbid certain behaviors even in your personal life—and there's that catch–all phrase of "conduct unbecoming" that just about covers anything that your CRJ employer can imagine that would be prejudicial to the agency. In short, if you engage in any behavior that is viewed as unethical, you can be fired.

With the field of criminal justice being as restrictive as it is, certain situations have made for interesting conversations with friends. Usually, they provide advice on how they would have done "this or that" if they were similarly situated. But as is the reality of the situation being as it was I explain why I am unable to react in a manner that they would since I am held to a different standard. The thing though, is that making these decisions is not "a drag" since *who* I am came first before I decided *what* I wanted to do for a living. If your assessment of all of these extra requirements for working in the field of criminal justice seem like a lot of trouble, it will probably feel even worse when you start the work. It is analogous to the concept espoused in home searches wherein it has been determined that if when you buy a new house and there is something important that you cannot ever change, such as the view – if it mildly irritates you from the start, your irritation will only grow into a nightmare over time if you elect to buy the house. If you think this will be easy for you, then you may enjoy working in the criminal justice field. But if you think it feels like something too hard to do when reading about it, try living it. You need to make an important distinction of whether the standards discussed are those you already hold yourself to, or if the standards feel oppressive because you would be forced to be held to the standard.

I recall a conversation with at least one person who was not pleased with my choice in a profession. I was asked if when my doctorate was completed if I were going to change my line of work. When I replied no, this person expressed such frustration that I had to know what was motivating this suggestion. I was told that a switch in professions was expected to result in me changing to the point that I would "loosen–up" and "lighten–up." I hope to this day that I was able to get this person to understand that "I am not who I am as a result of what I do, I have chosen this line of work because of who I am." So the reason that I do many of the things that I do have absolutely nothing to do with what I do, and has everything to do with who I am. You in turn need to examine yourself from a similar prospective. Knowing whether you find criminal justice standards as embracing or oppressing can help you determine if criminal justice is a good or bad fit for who you happen to be. Know that even under the best conditions wherein you embrace the standards; there will still be times when it will be hard. Your past and your future truly merge when it comes to breaking into and continuing in a field like criminal justice.

What kind of picture does your past paint? Is it a picture that you believe portrays to anyone looking a responsible person who is likely to make a good public servant? Or are there flaws? It has already been established that attempts at covering up should not be an option as failure to disclose is not a guarantee that no one will ever know. This would be quite a gamble when one considers that the element of worrying associated with being found out which could happen at any time. Moreover, should the worst happen—and "it" does get out, there is a possibility that after several years of personal investment in a job, you could be fired. Many criminal justice positions have "fine print" just above the signature line where you certify that the information contained in the application is true and correct to the best of your knowledge. There are sometimes even consequences mentioned in these documents in the event that any perjury is detected.

Does your past paint a picture of a person who has demonstrated trustworthiness, responsibility, reliability, and truthfulness which are all important qualities for public servants, especially those working in the field of criminal justice? If the answer is no, you should start thinking about what kinds of things you can do right now, to try and change that picture—so that when you are at the point of seeking employment, you will be in a much better position to obtain the job you want. What is the best way to ensure that you will be able to make it up to bat in the world of criminal justice? The answer to that question, which is to grasp as a guiding principle in life to "do the right thing" will not only help you come out okay during the hiring process, it will also carry you throughout your career. If that principle guides your decisions, even when you make mistakes, and we all do, you will recover. The mistakes will not be such that when viewed from a point in time backward that anyone will be able to say you were malicious in your intentions. But if one of your guiding principles is that you pledge with your heart to do the right thing, you are less likely to be in a situation where you are denied employment as a result of conduct in your past – stemming from your professional or personal life. The important principle of rightness is the cornerstone of Part IV designed to provide ethical guidance throughout your criminal justice career.

Part IV

You Got It!
Keep It!

Chapter 15

Beyond the Hiring Process: Keeping it Together

You would think after all it took to get that wonderful criminal justice position that the worst would be over. However, you will quickly discover that the sentiment on the street is true—namely, the same thing it took to get her (the job), is the same thing it takes to keep her (the job). Getting a professional position in the field of criminal justice necessitated that your life up to that point demonstrated evidence of high values and morals; keeping and advancing in your career requires the same commitment to making good decisions, exercising sound judgment, and behaving the right way.

This all sounds pretty easy, but the stakes are high. Anyone who has been in law enforcement for a number of years will tell you that no matter how good you are or how hard you work or how dedicated you are, all it takes is one poor decision to derail your career.[52] Whether that decision is later interpreted and adjudicated as corrupt, discriminatory, or abused power—all it takes is one time to result in dismissal or more serious sanctions. Even more sobering is the fact that many who find themselves in these unfortunate situations do not even know precisely how they ended up there.

I know of no one who decided to become corrupt or unethical. In many cases it was a gradual progression. I believe it can happen to just about anyone if they are not careful. How

---

[52] While still relatively rare, each year law enforcement officers are removed from their positions. The FBI's study of 107 agents who were dismissed, resigned or retired while under investigation for criminal and serious misconduct between 1986 and 1999 found less than one agent per thousand was dismissed during the period studied (Federal Employees News Digest, 2004).

many times have you lacked discipline and found yourself mindlessly doing something that you did not mean to? For me, if I do not constantly think about what over–eating can mean to my health and waist–line, I will actually seek out the cheese–cake. Ensuring an ethical CRJ career requires not only discipline but maintenance. This in turn requires CRJ professionals to periodically think about, talk about and practice doing the right thing. Part IV will provide a framework to facilitate a healthy mindset for sustaining an ethical CRJ career.

Chapter 16

Deciding to Do the Right Thing

Some time ago, a phrase jumped out at me on the radio that made me mad—mad enough that I immediately pondered and made record of it. I confess that I do not remember the context of the phrase which was undoubtedly attached to some advertisement and it is a good thing because I would have vowed right then and there not to buy whatever was being sold. The phrase went like this: "Be good, but if you cannot be careful." This statement gives all kinds of permissions to do wrong. In other words, if one chooses to do wrong, just be careful and what? Just do not get caught? I suspect that I may have been the only listener offended by the commercial's catchy phrase as it is indicative of a society that is casual about doing good and indeed the commercial's implication is that it may not even be possible. While American society as a whole may be more liberal, many of the agencies you seek to work for within the criminal justice system tend to hold more conservative ideologies necessitating that you develop a strong commitment to doing the right thing as early on as possible.

Although to do right is an action, it all starts in the mind. If you can get your head right, then I remain convinced that your decisions and thus your behavior will fall on the right side during your career in criminal justice. Before attempting to comprehend any specific standards for the field of criminal justice, you must grasp an ethical foundation for your life. If you do build an ethical base, every decision you make is likely to be well within the standards of conduct for any criminal justice position.[53] You should strive to have every decision that you make to be on the right side of "right."

---

[53] Even when your position requires unusual or challenging assignments, such as, undercover work, you can still remain ethical. I recall a debate I had with a member of the clergy whose percep-

Ethics is defined as conforming to the right standards of conduct for a given profession.[54] The emphasis is on the word "right." As stated, the standards of conduct for criminal justice professionals tend to be quite high. Some would argue that they are too high so much in fact that people find difficulty in meeting expectations and requirements. At times I have even heard complaints that a given person may not have known that what they were doing was wrong. However, I believe that we almost instinctively know when we are doing something right or wrong.

You can tell when you are contemplating doing something right or wrong. The test is two–fold: one is what is going on internally. Is what is pondered something that you feel proud about or is it something that you feel ashamed of? There are also all sorts of internal physical or psychological responses that are indicative signs of depression or elation corresponding to right or wrong behavior. These various internal feelings can tell you a lot about what you believe about a given behavior. In short, if you feel that you have done something that is right, you will feel good about it. If you have done something that you perceive is wrong or that you think you should not do, then you are not likely to feel good about it. Moreover, external cues also give you a secondary answer as to whether a decision and subsequent action was right or wrong.

I have noted that when people do something that they view is right, they are more likely to talk about it—some may even brag about it. How many of those bumper stickers do you see on cars of proud parents of students that make

---

tion was that undercover work was deceptive and wrong; but having engaged in a substantial amount of this type of work I see it more as a necessary acting role to bring about justice. However, there is no ambivalence within me relative to undercover work as I view it as a role necessary to conduct certain types of investigations that are dependant upon this technique.

[54] This is my favorite definition having used it for some 15 years; however, after having consulted every dictionary I own, I am of the opinion that it was derived as a combination of definitions I came across in dictionaries when I first began to teach Ethics.

"A's" ? Conversely, when a person has done something that they perceive is wrong, it is less likely that it will voluntarily be shared with others. The tendency is to conceal or hide the bad behavior[55] which more than likely is not going to be shared with anyone. You will want to conceal it—hide it. If one starts to think about ways to hide a given act before commission, indeed then it is probably something wrong and something that should be avoided. Using the bumper sticker example, I have yet to come across one bragging about offspring in prison. I rest my case that we usually know the difference between right and wrong based on internal and external indicators. But what of the reasons for doing either?

In my opinion, there is not much distance between doing the right thing for the wrong reasons or doing the wrong thing for the right reason and doing the wrong thing for the wrong reasons—wow pretty deep huh? The essence of what I am trying to convey here is that the motive behind what you do is just as important as what you actually do. It is not unusual when things go bad (i.e. alleged retaliation from EEO lawsuits, racial profiling, use of deadly force, etc), for criminal justice professional's motives to be questioned. The only defense to the scrutiny one must endure during times when one is on the defensive is having done the right thing and for the right reason. You need to develop a "moral compass" that is properly working for you at all times. Embracing the fundamentals of right thinking and behavior can assist you in more ways than one.

It has been said that an "honest man cannot be conned." I believe the reason this saying rings true is that if you are most concerned with doing right, you will not choose to do wrong simply because you believe you can make a quick

---

[55] I concede that there are people out there whose consciences have been self–altered to the point that when they have done something wrong they are oblivious to the fact; however I believe that they are in the minority. Moreover, among certain counter–culture groups, such as criminals, they may brag about wrong behavior—but hopefully it is not from this group that a candidate will enter the field of criminal justice.

buck. Situations and scenarios which may appear to be innocent on their face may actually cause you some major grief—and not just for purposes of getting a job in criminal justice. For example, I recall early in my career being approached by some people who seemed respectable trying to get me involved in a pyramid scheme. At the time, they did not even have a name for it; but what saved me was that it did not sound right. Moreover, I could not imagine harassing friends, family and neighbors to put their money into something that did not make sense either. You should take some time to familiarize yourself with cons that may save you a lot of heartache and complications in your profession.

As a criminal justice professional there is little defense for getting involved in cons and schemes whether as a "mark" (victim) or perpetrator. Con victim avoidance is important but unwittingly becoming a perpetrator in a confidence plot can land you in jail and minus assets you may have had previously. Even worse than unwitting schemes are situations where CRJ professionals intentionally defraud. Doing right could have saved the CRJ professionals listed below from the embarrassment and consequence associated with their fraudulent behavior (News, 2003):

• May 29, 2003, Loudonville, N.Y. — an attorney was formally disbarred after pleading guilty to three counts of insurance fraud. The attorney had pled guilty to insurance fraud, grand larceny and workers compensation fraud. He was charged with defrauding three insurers for more than $100,000.

• May 17, 2003, Floresville, Texas — The former head of the Poth police department was ordered to pay $1,000 fine and serve 10 days in jail for filing a fraudulent insurance claim on a patrol car. The judge also handed the former chief two years probation.

• May 8, 2003, Miami, Florida — A former Hialeah Police Department detective was arrested on charges that he filed several fictitious accident reports to create "patients" for a friend's medical clinic.

- May 1, 2003, Hanover Township, PA — Citing higher standards of behavior for law enforcement officials and saying he was setting an example, a federal judge in Scranton sentenced a former Hanover Township police officer to 10 months in prison for defrauding his car insurance agency.

Life Application Exercise #1

Hopefully, you are convinced that people know when they have done something right or wrong. However, to further illustrate this point and internalize the concept, do the following exercise that I employ in ethics workshops: Break up into groups consisting of three or more persons. Each small group is to meet and discuss the following.

- Group #1 develops a list of ways in which people react internally when they perceive they have done something right.

- Group #2 develops a list of ways in which people react externally when they perceive that they have done something right.

- Group #3 develops a list of ways in with people react internally when they perceive that they have done something wrong.

- Group #4 develops a list of ways that people react externally when they perceive they have done something wrong.

- Group #5 is to answer the question of whether or not the fact that *no one* will know about a particular behavior has the potential to influence decision–making or conduct. The answer should be supported by examples.

- Group #6 is to answer the question of whether or not the fact that *everyone* will know about a particular behavior has the potential to influence decision–making or conduct. The answer should provide examples to support the position taken.

- Group #7. Recognizing that ethics is conforming to the right standards of conduct for a given profession, create a list of the kinds of principles you can think of that are ethically right for a position you are considering.

- Group #8. Recognizing that ethics is conforming to the right standards of conduct for a given profession, create a list of the kinds of principles you can think of that are wrong for a CRJ position you are considering.

A spokesperson should be selected within each subgroup for representation when the entire group reassembles. The facilitator should have each spokesperson read the question and then relate the compiled list to the rest of the group for discussion.

I have found the responses to be uniform from workshop to workshop with a consensus that we all know the difference between right and wrong. Most of the feelings and behaviors listed fall into the categories of "head", "heart" or "gut." Perhaps a homogenous group consisting of criminal justice professionals yields similar results. However, I tend to believe that the uniformity is because the answers are universal to the American culture. How did your group stack up?

Life Application Exercise #2
(Ethical Dilemma)

A few years ago there was a situation involving law enforcement officers resulting in negative media for their department (Morrison: 2000).

In an effort to reduce the availability of illegal weapons, a campaign was launched by a criminal justice agency to purchase these guns – no questions asked. At some point it was discovered that many (one third) of the weapons surrendered for money came from law enforcement officers. It turned out that one of the highest ranking members of the department had entered into a swap of a weapon for money.

Additional information indicated that the officers were motivated to do this because they had obtained new guns rendering the swapped guns obsolete[56] from the standpoint of their usefulness as duty weapons. Moreover, these were weapons the officers had purchased with their own money.

Although there were "no questions asked," the program's administrators later posted signs making it clear that the officers' weapons were not welcomed in the exchange. Certainly the reporting of this fact in the newspaper discouraged the possibility that this would be repeated. Ask yourself the following questions:

1) Was the officers' conduct more right or more wrong?

2) Do you believe if the officers knew their actions would result in media attention, would they still have exchanged the guns for money? Do you believe there is a difference in decision—making based on negative media attention and the rank of the person making the decision?

3) Does the fact that they spent their own money have any effect on your opinion versus if these weapons had been paid for by the department?

4) These types of programs are frequently co—sponsored by another entity such as city counsel—how do you think the police department looked to the public they served during this time?

5) How do you think this situation should be handled?

---

[56] Starting in the late 1980s, many police departments went from using revolvers as duty weapons to semi—automatic handguns.

This life application exercise may also be role–played. Some of the recommended characters that could lead to relevant insight are the officers; the program's coordinator; chief of police; internal affairs; or city council member(s). The question could also be posed about whether the officers did the right thing from the various perspectives and an opening statement each of them would make on the subject.

How do you fare with other(s) participating in this exercise? I have facilitated lively group discussions with several criminal justice professionals[57] on this topic. Although, the most weighed mitigating circumstance considered is the fact that the officers used their own money to purchase the guns, it has been the opinion of these groups that the *intent* of the program, that was to remove *illegal guns*, meant that the officers should not have swapped their guns for cash in this situation.

---

[57] Some of the interesting points that came up are that participants are less harsh on the affected officers after learning that the officers paid for the weapons with their own money. In fact, this topic came up in a workshop I conducted with detectives from a police department who had personal friends involved in the scandal. And while admitting that I struggled with using this exercise with this particular group, by far it was the best debate I have facilitated thus far—I declare, during break I observed the detectives still discussing this issue.

Chapter 17

Rules, Rules, Rules

You Have Never Seen So Many Rules

It is recognized that since the field of criminal justice has several different positions, there may be many different individual ethics' documents guiding employee conduct; however, regarding them collectively there probably are many overlapping standards. To illustrate this point, the Department of Justice (DOJ) lists several elements/concepts as Standards of Conduct for its employees. These standards govern thousands of people which in some cases even extend to contractors and others that do business with this department of government. For example, all DOJ employees are expected to avoid conflicts of interest whereby their individual interests conflict with the best interests of the government. To ensure that this does not happen, strict guidelines are provided to DOJ employees for personal business practices to ensure that personal enterprises do not conflict with the government's business (DOJ: 2003)

In fact, if you examine just about any criminal justice code of ethics, you will find some limitations or restriction on how much business involvement employees many have with private entities that also engage in business with the employing agency. These are generally referred to as "conflict–of–interest" dealings. Most of us would likely agree that conflict of interest clauses are important to ensuring that governmental agencies have the confidence of its citizens that their decisions are objective. Consider for example, a recent situation reported whereby a District Attorney (D.A.) received campaign funds from a construction firm (Feldstein, 2003). What made the story newsworthy though is that the same company is being prosecuted for environmental crimes by the same D.A.'s office. Is not a concern of the citizenry that if this proves to be true, the outcome of the prosecution may not appear objective enough? Most of us would agree that conflict of interest statutes are to be expected; however, some of the rules governing CRJ employees are not as apparent.

The federal government is a large employer of criminal justice professionals in all branches of Government.[59] Conduct rules for federal employees are relatively strict which includes very specific prohibited behavior, such as, that employees shall satisfy in good faith all just financial obligations (Daniel, 2003). "It ought to be a crime" and in reality, for some agency restrictions, such as the aforementioned "voucher fraud" described are more than just rules, they may be illegal. Another act that is taboo for federal employees is the operation of official vehicles for personal use.[59] If it is proved that a federal employee used an official vehicle for personal use, by statute it must result in a 30 day suspension. No, not everyone is perfect[60] resulting in many federal employees having received an unpaid vacation for violating this rule.

The federal government routinely funds the transfer of its employees from one locale to another. Consequently, thousands of dollars are spent for each move. Government "orders" are cut similar to that of those in the military which outlines what federally appropriated dollars can be spent on identifying the employee and his or her dependants by name. Trust me, these orders are very specific. There are also documents that employees must sign acknowledging up front and later in voucher form after the move has taken place attesting to understanding of the regulations. One of the strict rules governing moves such as these is that those receiving the benefits are either the em-

---

[58] Employers in the executive branch include many agencies such as the FBI, DEA, and ATF&E; the legislative branch includes law makers such as Congressional representatives; and the judicial branch includes judges.

[59] 41 CFR 101-6.4 (NIH, 2002).

[60] Speaking of temptations! Stopping by the daycare on your way home to pick up your child in an official vehicle will earn you a 30-day suspension without pay.

ployee or the legally recognized dependants listed on the orders. Girlfriends, boyfriends or otherwise "significant others" (not spouses) residing with you before and after the move are not recognized. Some have seen this as unfair and found creative ways[61] of having the government finance such moves but if caught sometimes pay for it with termination of their jobs.

For some positions and agencies where and what you do after you leave can even be restricted. For example, it is prohibited to be involved in the official decision–making about a business an employee is planning to work for in the future. To ensure fairness and impartiality, the Department of Justice imposes a 1–2 year "cooling off" period (depending on position) for its employees to enter work for a company it had a government business relationship with prior to separation from the agency. Aside from the specific rules various CRJ agencies impose upon their employees, there are also general rules to fit just about any unethical behavior, even if it does not fit neatly into any category or even if the behavior is something not seen before.

One of the biggest catch–alls on rules is "conduct unbecoming." This essentially refers to behavior one may engage in that your friends or relatives might simply view as amusing, tacky or unseemly, but would find no reason to censure you for it. Whereas, as a criminal justice professional, you may be charged, disciplined or even dismissed for this same behavior, depending upon how severe it is considered, regardless of whether your activity occurred on or off duty. Another general conduct rule is, according to statute,[62] federal employees "shall not engage in criminal, infamous, dis-

---

[61] One such "creative case" that I am familiar with was of a male employee who was married to a female employee from the same agency. He was in the process of divorcing the female employee and had started cohabitation with his new girlfriend. During the course of all this, he was transferred. Since he was still married at the time of his transfer, he was entitled to have his spouse listed as a dependent. When the male employee was moved, he had his girlfriend's things moved as well. Later, when this whole scheme was uncovered by his employer – probably with a little help from his pending ex-wife, he was dismissed.

honest, immoral, or notoriously disgraceful conduct, or other conduct prejudicial to the government" (Daniel, 2003). For example, the situation described in an earlier section with regard to the pirating of music; while this matter is mostly being pursued as a civil matter, many CRJ employers may regard any scandal associated with its employees in this matter as unbecoming conduct resulting in possible charges and disciplinary action.

As you can see there are rules governing all kinds of actions for criminal justice positions that you may have never thought about. But the point is that you need to know what the standards of conduct that govern your particular position are so that you do not inadvertently violate them. Moreover, you need to ensure that your "moral compass" is working as most of what may be defined as unethical may not be defined in any specific agency rule or guideline. Consequences for violating the rules and regulations for CRJ positions can be quite steep as I have noted that for most criminal or even administrative offenses, regardless of how minor they may seem, carry substantial offenses. The range of punishment is usually from oral reprimand to dismissal. It would appear that CRJ employers want the latitude to make decisions based on the circumstances presented taking into account a given disciplinary record which would preclude commitment to a given sanction beforehand. So be careful.

Life Application Exercise #1

For the following set of behaviors, identify whether you would consider them to be conduct unbecoming a criminal justice professional. Try to view them from the standpoint of a criminal justice manager—so "should" will play a part in your thinking or discussion. Keep in mind that criminal justice professionals are generally held to a higher standard.

Behaviors:

---

[62] 5 CFR 735.203 (Daniel, 2003).

1) In the office building cafeteria, an employee yells at the cashier because she takes too long to ring up the order.

2) Reading a co–worker's personal mail which was already unopened and in plain view.

3) Spreading a story about the boss that seems to be untrue.

4) Having an extra–marital sexual relationship.

5) Unmarried, but cohabitating.

6) Not paying bills.

7) Snatching identification from the hand of an individual the employee initially allowed examining.

You probably figured out that each of the above, depending on mitigating or aggravating factors may be construed as conduct unbecoming for a criminal justice professional. The purpose of the exercise is to assist you in your critical thinking about behavior you might previously have only thought just may be part of a "bad hair day"—but know this, depending on how extreme the situation may become, the more likely one may face serious after–effects. Consider for example scenario #7 described above actually occurred between an off–duty officer of one agency when he was stopped by police from another agency. During this altercation which escalated into an argument, and struggle, the off duty officer was arrested. This altercation received media attention on a national level and at least one television program showed what occurred during (it was caught on tape) and afterwards legally. What struck me the most about this case was how embarrassing it was to the entire law enforcement community. How can public confidence be expected when cops will not even extend the courtesies to each other that they demand of others? Criminal justice professions should always endeavor to de–escalate any situation rather than escalate it. We have seen many examples of just how far a matter may go out of control when cooler heads do not prevail.

Much of what happens to you from a discipline standpoint is determined by who finds out, and whether a given offense is part of something bigger. Your discipline record also is usually factored in when decisions are being made about sanctions. If faced with a situation where you are charged, you should be truthful in your discussions for several reasons to include possible impeachment as a witness in future court appearances as a result of having given false statements in the past.

What of your friends and foes? It will not take long for them to determine that you have a job which makes you vulnerable in your off–duty conduct. Consequently, you should endeavor to study the code of ethics or principles of conduct provided to you by your employer very early in your career to help guide you in behaving appropriately. I have noted this to be particularly a problem when someone you previously viewed as in your corner suddenly is no longer there—such as an ex–spouse. They often become the source of disclosing all sorts of secrets that ultimately can result in the undoing of one's career—another reason to walk the straight and narrow at all times. Do not give your enemies an opportunity to speak ill of you.

Life Application Exercise #2

A detective intends to retire within the next two years. His plans for retirement involve working in the private sector using skills and contacts he has made along his law enforcement career. Recognizing his plan, the detective starts being especially nice to possible prospective employers. For example, in the case of one company owner he knows that has began wooing him to work for after retirement, using his discretion, the detective gives that particular business extra work to the exclusion of other companies providing the same service (it is recommended, but not required by his employer that the department obtains this service on a rotating basis among the few qualified businesses). Moreover, the detective also calls other detectives whose responsibility is to coordinate these services in their respective areas and starts bad–mouthing the other companies suggesting the he has found Company X's services to be superior. Not surprisingly, when the detective retires, he starts working for Company X. Did the detective do anything wrong? Do you believe this is a conflict of interest for the detective? Do you believe it *should* be a conflict of interest for the detective?

Chapter 18

Do Criminal Justice Professionals Have Freedom of Speech?

The question of how free your speech remains after becoming a criminal justice professional is debatable. While the U.S. Constitution gives every citizen the right to freedom of speech, you may be asked to give up some of this right upon accepting employment. Criminal justice agencies cannot afford to permit employees to disclose any and every thing at will. There does exist confidential information that agencies generally guard.

Agencies expect that your public speech will not convey a position contrary to the organization's missions and goals. Consider the following scenario:

"In what appears to be a case of extremely bad timing, a Billings man at the center of a national debate over freedom of speech says he lost his job after a story about the case appeared in The Gazette.....In 2002, he was convicted of felony possession of a half–gram of psilocybin mushrooms and was sentenced to three years probation. His conviction prompted an interest in drug reform laws and he organized a Billings chapter of the National Organization for the Reform of Marijuana Laws, or NORML. He planned a concert to "raise money for an initiative to place the legalization of medicinal marijuana on the 2004 ballot.....A story about the concern appeared in Gazette on June 14. Three days later (the man) lost his job....." (Fitzgerald, 2003).

In the aforementioned case, the man insists he was fired because of his beliefs while the employer maintains he was not. However, a word to the wise, when your ideology conflicts with your agency's mission, and you speak out to the press about it, there is bound to be trouble. Moreover, your employer will not likely take kindly to your making statements that may be embarrassing.

No matter how accurate your statements may be, public criticism of your employer is not likely to be welcomed. Soldiers serving in the Iraqi war faced discipline as a result of negative statements they made about the Secretary of Defense's alleged reneging on a promise to permit their return home on at least two occasions. In response to the "grumbling and whining" to reporters, some military officials were pursing charges of insubordination (Friedman, 2003).

Your employer generally expects that you will not profit from information obtained while discharging your official duties, not known or available to the general public. For example, federal "employees shall not engage in financial transactions using non–public information, or allow the improper use of non–public information to further any private interests" (Daniel, 2003). This was the ethics standard that I had to be most mindful of as I wrote this book. Obviously I have access to much information not known or available to the general public. Thus, this was my standard – anything that was not known or available to the public was not included. In very public cases, it may be thought that the public knows much but the thirst for more always seems to be there. Such was the case in the sniper serial killings occurring in Maryland and Virginia in 2002.

Former Montgomery County Police Chief Charles Moose, a very public figure during the shootings decided to write a book about the case before even the trials commenced. In response, the Montgomery County Ethics Commission forbid Chief Moose from telling his story about the serial killings occurring in 2002 in movie or book[63] form. It was asserted that Chief Moose was attempting to profit from the prestige of his office (American Police Beat, 2003).

---

[63] The book, Three Weeks in October was published in 2003.

Chief Moose resigned shortly after this ruling and was expected to pursue book and movie deals.

Life Application Exercise

Refer back to the story about the guy who lost his job after there were newspaper accounts about his drug conviction and subsequent press about his efforts to get legislation passed on drug legalization. The employee was quoted as stating that he "couldn't pass the background check, they never put the application in....I became a liability because of my political beliefs." Recognizing that our beliefs affect our behavior, do you believe that those holding certain beliefs should refrain from certain jobs whose ideology may conflict with the agency's goals and objectives? The private industry employer was quoted as stating "what people do when they're off the job is their business." However, if he were a criminal justice professional, would this situation have been his employer's "business"? Would his firing based on information obtained from the press have been justified?

As a criminal justice professional what you say can also have more weight and hence more consequences than the average Joe or Jane. You really never know who may be listening to a conversation. If you strive to never say anything you do not mind having overheard by others or something told in confidence being repeated, you will less likely make an embarrassing statement that can lead to creating professional difficulties. Two situations come to mind that illustrate this professional dilemma: Mark Furman, the Los Angeles detective alleged to have made racial slurs as testified about at the O.J. Simpson trial and Governor Rick Perry of Texas whose recorded comments made during a traffic stop were used as fodder by his opponent in the Gubernatorial election in 2002.

Chapter 19

Competency

Do you believe how well someone is able to do their job is or should be a question of ethics? Is there a minimal level of performance wherein if a person falls below, the individual and his/her supervisor should consider discontinuation in that field? The police academy experience provided me with a framework for pondering this question. Having been both trainee[64] and instructor, I regard competency assessment as an issue worthy of review from beginning and throughout a CRJ career. The academy is the gateway location for law enforcement positions in that while it may not be the only place to gauge whether a person has the aptitude and skill necessary to engage in this kind of work—it certainly presents an opportunity for many staff to observe a trainee from different vantage points to access ability.

In my positions of management, counseling and mentoring, I frequently seek to determine whether low performance is a product of a person's *unwillingness* to improve or *inability* to improve. I have posed the question several times regarding performance which is not up to par—namely is the individual's poor performance a product of his/her unwillingness to do better or an inability to do better? I ask this question because usually if you are dealing with someone who *will not* do what is required, it may be more of an attitude problem. And we know that attitude is everything. Conversely, if the issue involves something one *cannot* do, oftentimes it has something to do with capacity or ability and ultimately affects competency.

Everyone was not meant to do everything. And sometimes no matter how hard a person tries, he or she will not be able to do certain things. I find that it has been more difficult as a manager to deal with the person who can't do the

---

[64] I have attended two separate police academies.

job as opposed the person who won't do the job. Regardless of why performance is low, the answer to the problem is to bring the person up to standard. The person with the attitude problem can be counseled into improvement if he or she is willing to change. Whereas, the person who cannot do better—probably due to him/her being mismatched to a job he or she wanted but physical, intellectual or other limitations prevent them from doing better. It can be heart–breaking to see one person "who has got it all" take abilities for granted when there is another who will work with a good attitude as hard as he may and still not be up to par.

The key is that we must all know when to say when. If you determine that you are not capable of doing your job, you have an obligation to not engage in the work because in the field of criminal justice you may be putting yourself at risk as well as others. I have found that competence issues usually are revealed—and quickly. It is probably better to examine one's self closely and self–assess abilities and performance. If we determine that we are incapable of doing a job at an acceptable level, no matter how hard we try—ethics and integrity dictates that we try another position. Resignation is usually more advantageous[65] than being fired—and it gets your supervisor off the hook for having to take action that he or she is not likely to derive any pleasure.

Assuming that those who can not perform well in a criminal justice position are in the minority, we can agree that much of competency has to do with employees simply applying themselves. In other words—doing their jobs. For example, years ago when I was conducting research on violence directed at witnesses I came across a case which made me shudder. A woman had agreed to cooperate with

---

[65] It also will look better when you are seeking other employment. Just because you are not able to do one job in the field of criminal justice does not mean that you cannot do another job. I have seen for example many cases where people starting out in law enforcement positions change careers within the same agency for jobs just as rewarding and with comparative pay.

the D.A.'s office in the investigation of her boyfriend. The letter which outlined her plea agreement was mistakenly addressed to and mailed to her boyfriend. Shortly after he obtained the letter he shot her, but fortunately she was not mortally wounded. This story illustrates how important it is that those working in the criminal justice field, regardless of position are competent including an attentiveness to detail.

I believe that it is impossible to be attentive to what is going on when one is sleeping. Recently I was moving through an airport which required a secondary identification check. As was protocol, the airport employee escorted me to the officer's booth (which was opaque) where he made repeated attempts (knocking and calling) to get the officer's attention to no avail. Finally, the airline employee had to jump up above the booth area to rouse the officer from slumber. It is a good thing that nothing happened during this time which would have required the officer to react to. It did not completely surprise me in my subsequent conversation with the embarrassed officer his revelation that he was very close to retirement—indeed it would appear that he has already gotten a head start. This incident did not become public meaning doubt is not cast upon his department based on his actions. However, an airline pilot was not so fortunate.

A recent illustration of the importance of ethical behavior and how it may bear on perception of your competency concerned an airline pilot caught by passengers sleeping on the job (Ross, 2003). In addition to the safety implications of this behavior, his actions also were embarrassing for his employer likely to have an effect on the airline's reputation. Reputation is important to private and pubic agencies. As in the case of the airline pilot, there is a safety issue associated with "sleeping on the job" and it can also adversely affect the reputation of the agency.

I submit that there is a given standard employees in criminal justice agencies must strive for to secure the confidence of tax paying citizens. No agency can afford a crisis of confidence. Those entering the field of criminal justice must be willing to self–assess and make necessary adjustments to make certain they are up to the challenge of these important public servant positions. Your competency is critical and can place the entire reputation of your agency in question extending to fulfilling its mission. For example, an apparent lack of competency on the part of employees at a forensic laboratory resulted in the lab's closure and now employees face the possibility of sanctions (McVicker, 2003).

Life Application Exercise #1

It is not uncommon when unethical behavior on the part of criminal justice professionals becomes public and known to family or friends either by news account or personal experience that you are confronted. It's an occupational hazard that if you are one of "them," you must at least be able to provide some deeper insight into the behavior. When you are faced with these "inquests," what is your normal response? Do you usually automatically take the position of family or friends or the criminal justice professional? Or do you take your own position based on your own knowledge of the facts? Do you convey this independent position to others, or secretly keep your opinion to yourself? If yes, what is the benefit of doing either?

I know how sticky these discussions can get with colleagues as well as friends and family. I worked in New York City during two very public and controversial cases[66] which generated lots of discussions. However, I did notice that the conversations were in clusters of persons who shared like positions, as opposed to a mixed debate. A good thing, I believe because very heated discussion would have ensued. I was also a law enforcement officer during unveiling of the

---

[66] The trial in 2000 wherein a police brutality case resulted in officers' convictions of torturing Abner Louima occurred while I was in New York as well as the incident involving the shooting of unarmed suspect Amadou Diallo 41 times by police.

highly controversial O.J. Simpson verdict where there was much heated debate although I did not witness any change in opinions.

Life Application Exercise #2

Romantic "affairs" while distasteful have been the downfall of some CRJ professionals. Recently a FBI agent was reported resigning under pressure after it was disclosed that he had had a romance with the wife of a mobster that he had previously been assigned to protect (Malinowski, 2003). Pretend that you are a CRJ employee who has become more and more suspicious about the conduct of a co–worker. The co–worker seems to have developed an intimate personal relationship with an ex–con turned informant. You believe this because the male co–worker and the female informant kid around with each other a lot and are touching more and more in their communications. Next, one night when you are out socially you run into the co–worker and the informant having drinks together and no work activity is scheduled at the time. A week later, your co–worker attempts to get you to exaggerate the informant's performance to the boss to increase a payment amount. Things deteriorate to the point that all doubt is removed about the nature of your co–worker and the informant's relationship as you catch the informant sharing payment received with the co–worker. This behavior is regarded as a violation of the standards of conduct for your agency. At what point will you do anything? What will you do?

There is an old saying when there is damage control after an incident has occurred and in assessing blame; it goes something like this: "What did you know; when did you know it; and what did you do about it?" And for those situations where there is an issue involving competency, you may very well apply that test to yourself. What was it that I knew at the time and when did I know it? What did I do about it? There may come a time when you may need to defend your actions. Obviously, hindsight is "20–20" where determining a best course of action is as clear as day. But the important question at the time, with the limited knowledge that you possessed will be the gauge used to judge the decision. If you find yourself in a position and you are trying to sort things out, ask yourself those questions. What you do can be important in the sense the sooner you perceive there is a requirement for action the sooner you would be expected to act. Being committed to action will save you on many occasions as a CRJ professional. Failure to act in many ways can be worse than taking actions later determined to have been inferior.

Chapter 20

Abuse of Power

Do you know someone who when temporarily placed in charge seems to let it "go to his/her head?" I think we all do. Quite frankly, it is frightening that when these types are in charge, and frequently from a relatively stable environment, chaos emerges. When decisions are based on selfish motives tinged with immaturity, usually the decisions are not likely to be in the best interest of the organization, nor for the individuals the organization is expected to serve or protect. There is a problem with persons who abuse power in positions of authority.

It should be taken into consideration that law enforcement and related occupations place even entry level personnel in positions to wield much power. In between law enforcement jobs, I worked in a job as a director and supervisor—a job with much potential. In deciding whether to pursue that line of work, or return to law enforcement, I must confess, a factor I was guided by was the realization that in the management job I had no real power. Once I made a decision that my boss clearly supported me in only to learn that she had been over–ruled by her superiors rendering my initial decision null and void.

In contrast, as I reflected on my days as a street cop, my decisions counted and essentially were final. How I handled a given incident was how it was to be and other entities, such as, my supervisor, the department as a whole, prosecutors and so on—all had to live with my decision(s). Now while this gave me satisfaction, it is also a humbling experience knowing that the consequences of one's actions in an instant can have reverberating consequences for a long time, and affect many people. The flip side is that with having your decisions final also is a tremendous responsibility.

In addition to power, criminal justice professionals have a degree of discretion in discharging their duties as well as opportunities to learn private things about people that the general public does not usually enjoy. Where abuse of power can be manifested in connection with discretion could be in taking legal action (i.e. arrest or prosecution) for people with certain characteristics (i.e. based on beauty, race, gender, socio economic condition, etc.), but making opposite decisions for those not similarly situated. For example, there has been much research in criminology about the alleged "paternal" reaction to female criminal offenders said to contribute to their receiving lighter sentences than their male counterparts.

Equality

The sensitive subjects of racism, sexism, and EEO (equal employment opportunity) involve the issue of ethics. Treating others fairly and equitably without regard to race, ethnicity, gender, religion, age or other non–behavioral characteristics should be a goal for all criminal justice professionals to strive towards. Not only is discrimination an ethical issue, but frequently it is a legal issue as well. Equality, or the perceived lack thereof is a foundational issue in that many police–community relation problems can be identified relating to it (i.e. abuse of power, racial profiling, excessive force, etc.). Why things are this way is a subject for another book; however, for our purposes identifying how to behave ethically in this area will be our focus.

First of all, I believe that part of the problem that we have in this area is an unwillingness to admit that there is a problem, let alone dealing with it. This has resulted in many underprivileged groups fighting for rights. And with an emphasis on "fighting," it is not hard to see how parts of the CRJ system may seem at odds with certain groups while at the same time its employees feeling at odds as well. If you ask most CRJ professionals, they will advise you that they are not prejudiced and yet evidence that something is wrong is all too apparent. I have come to notice sometimes when people are engaging in discriminatory practices, they do not even know it; behavior is unconscious. I will give you an example:

As a supervisor I had an individual come in once
and say to me that he was very excited about working
with one individual from another agency because of
that person's ethnic background—he believed that
person would be able to assist us in a unique way with
cases involving individuals from the same ethnic
background as the newcomer. For example, the lan-
guage issue—he would be able to translate; and this
person could give us some insight on the culture.
Then this worker went on to say that in spite of the
fact that he was excited about this individual working on the team with us that he was concerned—the
same thing that he was pleased about, he was concerned in that he believed that this person's ethnic
background predisposed that individual to crime because he had seen so many of this particular group
engaged in crime—so he asked me if arrangements
could made to do a special check on this individual so
he could assuage his worry that this individual was a
criminal also.

While this discriminatory perception and attempt
to get me to also engage in discrimination was glar-
ing, I pushed the envelope in my questioning in hopes
that something would click in his thinking so he
would realize that this would be a discriminatory
practice if I agreed to it. And realizing that this guy
just did not have a clue, I begin to take it to an almost
absurd extreme to try and identify at some point if he
would pick up on the fact that this would be discriminatory behavior. But I have to tell you that I learned
that his threshold was endless as I began to say
things like: well we are going to have other people
that you will work with from other agencies—would
you like for me to do additional checks on them and he
said no, no, just this person. Next, I reminded him
that this person does work for this other agency
where they would have done some checks on him already with him responding but you know after all he
is one of *those* people adding that "they" are not to be

trusted which is why he said he wanted to do these additional checks.

When after I had taken it to the extreme and no light eventually went off, I then explained to him very calmly, not trying to demean him, the reasons that I could not do what he was asking me to do. And while he looked very bewildered when he left my office I really believe even though he clearly intended to discriminate in this situation if I had let him, he had no knowledge that anything was wrong with the practice he was proposing.

This story illustrates the fact that sometimes discrimination is based on a lack of education and people not thinking which is frequently why people engage in these practices.

Sometimes people discriminate unconsciously without realizing that what they are doing is wrong or illegal. I think that is why it is imperative that CRJ training is presented in a manner to help sensitize persons to biases and what constitutes discrimination. Hopefully you will obtain training in this area, but even if you do not you should "self–train." You can do this by studying the laws, practices and polices and committing to apply them consistently and fairly without regard to race, creed, color, national origin and the other characteristics protected under the EEO laws. Moreover, examining yourself for individual bias will help you tremendously in identifying which areas you may have to work harder at to avoid unintended discrimination.

Many civil servants have quite a bit of discretion as it relates to their area of responsibility. Law enforcement officers can exercise options, especially in the case of misdemeanors for making decisions of whether or not they will make an arrest. They can make decisions as to whether or not they are going to issue tickets. Probation and parole officers have discretion in whether or not they believe they should return someone back to prison. Recognizing that there is so much discretion among CRJ professionals, it is essential that you exercise that authority consistently and fairly. If you examine decisions that you have made in the past and you find that some of those decisions appear to be based on factors other than behavior, you need to proceed cautiously. None of the suggestions made will be helpful though if it is not acknowledged that discrimination is really a problem.

I have attended several meetings where EEO is the topic of conversation. While these meetings are designed to sensitize employees, the overwhelming sentiment seems to be hesitancy on the part of participants that discrimination actually exists. The most vocal in the group attempt to prove their case in the following manner: First, there is the question posed about the frequency of EEO complaints being filed. Next, to demonstrate that whatever number is supplied is not valid or can be further reduced comes the accusation that since the majority of the cases do not result in a finding of discrimination, that there is no discrimination; and finally, should not those who filed these complaints "wrongly" be charged in some manner for submission of frivolous cases? With this reaction to EEO training it is not surprising that those who perceive to have been discriminated against frequently also perceive and often prove retaliation in response to the initial complaint.

What needs to be understood on this issue is that just because a person was not able to prove that discrimination occurred does not mean that it did not occur. Moreover, the number of complaints filed do not define the true universe of instances of discrimination any more so than the reporting of and convictions of criminal offenses is a true representation of all crime committed. With that said, I believe that training in this area should focus more on our perceptions and our behavior and helping us to understand that certain reactions are to be expected and it is more important that we over–ride these "default" emotions. For example, I believe that it is a normal emotional reaction to become outdone when someone makes an accusation that a decision was based on one thing when you know that it is not. Oftentimes when a complaint of discrimination is made known, an individual will attribute a decision of a manager to be based upon race or gender or religion when the manager feels that well, yes I made that decision but it was not based on any of these types of things and so automatically that individual who is alleged to have discriminated is not pleased with the employee and sometimes will begin to *react* by treating that employee differently, even if the original complaint was unfounded. It is natural to feel resentment, but this emotion must be kept in check to avoid retaliating against persons who regardless of how misguided they may be have a legal right to pursue concerns they may have regarding equality. Aside from allegations of discrimination which may occur within a CRJ agency, at times discrimination is alleged from outside of the agency.

Although not all–exclusive in the search for equality, the concept of "racial profiling" has recently become a hot subject in policing. Racial profiling, defined as stopping a person based solely on race or ethnicity instead of an individualized suspicion arising from the person's behavior (BJS, 2001) has been a concept existing for a long time. It seemed to have been particularly evident in the early 1980s as blacks were singled out for scrutiny in cases where they were observed riding in expensive vehicles by police who stopped them. It was not until the late 1990s when several critical incidents resulted in this phenomenon raising the consciousness of the nation. Since that time, many agencies have published new polices providing guidance to their employees to avoid situations of racial profiling. However, the guidance is just that. As to whether an individual will be singled out due to physical attributes instead of behavior is completely up to the discretion of the criminal justice professional making the intervention.[67]

---

[67] I believe that criminal justice professionals besides police can initiate contacts with the public inappropriately. I personally, in my role as a law enforcement officer have been challenged by other criminal justice professionals based simply on my appearance. In one instance, I was in a court room guarding persons under arrest. When the defendants were ordered to rise, the magistrate looked at me and asked if I understood his order for defendants to rise. A colleague explained to the judge that I was not a defendant. This magistrate, by the way is a person I hold in high regard, but you see my point that well meaning people can make decisions based

The lesson for the prospective criminal justice major to learn from racial profiling scandals is that we all have biases which need to be identified and dealt with. Consequences for not doing so can be substantial. Consider for example the resigning of two officers who were being investigated as a result of a video tape discovered of a traffic stop they had made. "The tape depicts the troopers yelling racial epithets at the occupants of the vehicle. The tape shows one of the troopers finding a bag of drugs, but the officer is then seen stomping on the bag of drugs instead of taking it in as evidence" (American Police Beat, 2003).

Individuals who engage in illegal discrimination can make not only their own lives difficult but also place their agencies' future at great peril. Consider for example the many cases of alleged racial profiling by certain police departments that have resulted in assignment of a federal monitor. One case occurred in 1999, when a federal monitor was put in place to oversee a State Police Department found by the courts to have engaged in racial profiling. Perhaps the most troubling account described in that case was the shooting of unarmed minority college students during a traffic stop resulting in three of the students being wounded. It was later admitted that the students were stopped because police officers were informed by supervision that minorities were more likely to be involved in drug trafficking (Public Agenda Online, 2002). In addition to the federal monitor, and the 12.9 million dollar award[68] to the victims in this case, the damage to this police department's reputation was substantial.

---

on characteristics instead of behavior which is why we could all work on this.

Another situation occurred as I traversed through a court house area during the course of bail hearings. This time one of the prosecutors, assuming I was there to seek release for a friend or family member, asked me to identify my significant other among the defendants.

[68] The cost of police misconduct to a city can be substantial. Another city was reported to have paid a cumulative total of roughly $176.9 million to dispose of more than 3,500 police misconduct cases over a 16 year period (McCoy, 2000). has to be dealt with.

The current problem America faces in what to do about the perceived terrorist threat of certain illegal aliens in the country is also a consequence of racism.[69] If racial profiling had not been such a prolific phenomenon in our country, then outrage at its existence would have been non existent; hence, no one would now have a basis for debating the parallels between a security policy in reaction to the attacks on September 11, 2001 which has some merit in logic with a procedure that does not. It becomes hard to explain to people how things are different when racism lingers as was illustrated in the aforementioned example concerning racial profiling.

In studying the issue of race, crime and criminal justice intervention, I believe that while there are a few CRJ professionals in the minority who may be racist, as is the case in the general population, I believe that the majority of CRJ professionals are not. I would even venture to say that the few CRJ employees found to have engaged in racial profiling or other types of discrimination do so much more out of ignorance than any malicious intent. That is why I recommend strongly that as a matter of improving your competency and complying with the law, in addition to self–training you should interact with persons different from yourself. Courses have been designed to assist the U.S. workforce with sensitizing to different cultures in an effort to improve diversity and harmony. Failure to do this, I believe has a direct bearing the incidence of excessive force in a given community.

Police brutality, a topic often broached from the standpoint of discrimination is another form of abuse of authority. It has been a frequent complaint by minorities within the U.S. that they have disproportionately been subjects of excessive force. Indeed, there have been many findings of courts in the nation demonstrating that at times police use excessive force in the performance of their duties. Some of the larger departments have particularly been scandalized

---

[69] In listening to reactions on racial profiling, I sometimes wonder if some people are more upset about its existence or the fact that it has to be dealt with.

by the actions of a few of their officers. One city paid out $16.3 million to settle 25 civil cases involving brutality or other wrongdoing (McCoy, 2000).

Fortunately, the tide has changed in this nation with respect to police brutality. There was a time when a police officer could beat a suspect and get away with it. There was a time when officers could beat their spouses without repercussions. But with both of these serious social issues coming more into the forefront, each is less tolerated. Legal action, laws and massive pay outs have gotten the attention of police departments resulting in less tolerance by executives. No longer sweeping such situations under the rug, police departments now seem motivated to eliminate hiring and retaining officers prone to engage in excessive force.

As in the case of other forms of discrimination, I believe that study of one's self can also minimize the incidence of excessive force. Having reviewed very public cases of where police have been particularly brutal, I believe that as many of them have declared—there is real fear of the citizenry officers are expected to protect. When people are not familiar with other cultures it is easier to misread and misinterpret actions to be harmful when in reality they are not. Again, the more study of and interaction one has with other cultures, the less likely that these misinterpretations would expect to occur.

Unethical Behavior and the Code of Silence

A condition which contributes significantly to many unethical acts being perpetrated is the climate of the locale in which it occurs. In other words, how others react to an occurrence of misbehavior conducted in their presence can predict how comfortable perpetrators will feel in engaging in misdeeds which undoubtedly affects its incidence and prevalence. I could never condone keeping quiet about co—workers engaging in criminal behavior in my presence. I have been fortunate enough not to have ever observed any serious misconduct. However, I attribute this to several factors such as not working in a criminal-prone environment (thus there is less opportunity for observation), but also I attribute it as much to the fact that I carry myself in a manner that I want anyone who is thinking about engaging in criminal behavior to be uncomfortable around me. They, not I should be the uncomfortable ones. I want anyone contemplating misdeeds to feel as though there is no doubt that if they choose to go crazy and steal something with me around that I will similarly lose my mind also and report them. I think a proactive, offensive approach goes a long way in terms of what people will do in your presence.

To this day I remain confused about the existence of "the code of silence" within many law enforcement agencies. Would a criminal justice professional be expected to keep silent about some illegal activity he/she observed a criminal engaged in? The answer is no. That is why it is so confusing if you think about why a criminal justice professional would consider keeping quiet[70] about illegal behavior he observes a criminal colleague engaged in. There really is not much difference between the two cases other than detection and labeling. In the case of the known criminal, the subculture expects reporting whereas, some who do not readily make the distinction are reluctant to turn in criminals with credentials. This should not happen.

Ultimately, the criminal with credentials will be found out—the question is whether it will occur by those outside or within the criminal justice field. Obviously, the agency's reputation as well as that of its employees will fare far better if the offending is detected and handled by those within the agency as opposed to outside of it. Burris (1999) suggests that if police departments create an incentive for officers to report misconduct and resist the customs of police misconduct, the blue wall of silence can be broken.

---

[70] I just got something in the mail that may have some bearing on reporting misconduct of co–workers. It was a notice included in my government credit card bill urging report to the Inspector General's Office of anyone that misuses his or her government charge card.

What should you do when your values clash with that of your employer or managers within your agency? If you have been on your job for a while, it is likely that some of what you experience, is a result of the culture at your organization. Burris (1999: 213–214) writes:

> "What lives in the heart of a man or woman, is planted by the culture in which they are immersed. And if the heart of a culture is corrupt or indifferent or biased, the hearts of its members will be swayed in that direction. On the other hand, if the heart of a culture is open, fair, and respectful, that seed will take root and, eventually, will grow in all of its members."

Staying put, places you in a position to effect change more than being on the outside ever does. You should factor into your decision–making whether the value leads to illegal behavior. But what if you are the issue? What if virtually every section you have read suggests that you need to have your values strengthened in some way? I have made policy recommendations to any that will listen that when serious integrity breeches occur, remedial ethics should be part of the reckoning package. If there is remedial driver's training for personnel who are at fault in accidents and firearms, remedial for accidental discharges of a weapon, with decision–making being so important; why not have remedial ethics? And so, recognizing that this book is all about you, if you find yourself in a situation where you are slipping, *you* should confidentially seek counseling in an effort to reinforce values that are required to make decisions with integrity that will lead to ethical behavior.

I would like to tell you that all those who work in criminal justice agencies have higher moral standards than those in other organizations—but of course this in not necessarily true.[71] Moreover, a failure to get some people to come around to the ethics of criminal justice has really been

---

[71] Although I believe that criminal justice agencies, law enforcement in particular, have ethical standards that suggest the goal is to elevate the conduct of their employees above the general public.

to give up instead of allowing people to make wrong decisions. For example, some criminal justice agencies had to remove the option of decisions which could result in misconduct. After the advent of the 900 phone lines where sex talk is sold, many law enforcement agencies simply blocked their business telephone lines from being able to make these calls. Similarly, Causey (2003) reports that at one agency, officials had to block transactions with more than 300 businesses after employees were found to have used government credit cards for products or services not needed or used at the office.

The long and short of it is that integrity is the responsibility of each and every criminal justice professional. Agencies can set controls in place to reduce the likelihood that CRJ professionals will engage in misbehavior due to increased detection and or sanctions, but ultimately keeping ethically fit is an individual responsibility. You can choose not to abuse your authority as a CRJ professional if awareness exists. Thus, I recommend a self–evaluation periodically, especially since abuse of power is something which can result in serious consequences. I think a gauge for keeping oneself from abusing authority is to recognize it as the awesome responsibility that it is to be taken seriously rather than a personal tool to be used at will.

Life Application Exercise #1

Review news stories and popular movies with themes on abuses of power. Evaluate others' actions so you can assess your thinking on this topic. Do you find yourself focusing on how wrong and negative the villain's behavior was and associated negative consequences to him/her and the agency or wondering why the offender was not smarter in his choices to avoid detection?

Life Application Exercise #2

Which type of personality characteristics displayed below do you believe may be associated with engaging in excessive force:

a) Those who bully; or

b) "nice people" who do whatever is asked of them.

In my experience, both of these extreme personalities have difficulty with excessive force. The bully for obvious reasons, and the "go–along" types because they are easily influenced and are prone to doing whatever the dominants in the group do and or maintain the code of silence.

Life Application Exercise #3

Would you be tempted to use your authority inappropriately? Daily News, Tuesday, November 30, 1999 entitled "Stocks Scammers to Repay $450 Grand." This a case involving a Supreme Court Sergeant who was involved with people engaged in a scam where individual citizens were investing monies in a business empire which collapsed and this Sergeant encouraged people to put their money into. After being charged, he pled guilty to larceny and was sentenced to about one year in jail. What is interesting is that he met these individuals while he was working on a case. So he knew that they were criminals apparently ignoring the general prohibition against associating with criminals. I guess my point here is to make sure that you understand that regardless of whatever position you consider in the criminal justice field, there will be opportunities for bribery or to engage in other types of corruption. And the sergeant knew that the people he got involved with were criminals and he used his position as an opportunity to meet and work in a criminal enterprise conspiring to defraud and steal from citizens.

Life Application Exercise #4[72]

Many who think that minorities engage in crime more than others probably will continue to do so unless they take some time to really think the situation over. However, whereas before this bias could drive someone's discretionary decision–making (i.e. who to stop and investigate), now departments have provided guidelines that are "behavior based" removing discretionary individual guidelines which may have been race–based.

Which officer do you believe will have the most difficult time following departmental dictums concerning racial profiling:

a) the officer who previously unconsciously engaged in the practice, but who now believes it is wrong? Or

b) the officer who believes that minorities do commit more crime, but does not want to get into trouble so he vows to focus on behavior before making discretionary stops?

When it is all said and done if the unethical behaviors described become part of one's life, such as abuses of authority, failure to follow rules and regulations, or constantly choosing to do the wrong thing, misconduct can lead to corruption. Reinforce your values as needed. Before anyone else will ever know about you slipping off the deep end and spiraling down the slippery slope, you will know. If you feel yourself getting out of control and tempted to do things you never thought of—get HELP. Your establishing some kind of accountability with someone even if they do not work where you do will help you keep on the straight and narrow.

---

[72] A good test on racial bias is presented in Burris (1999), pages 209–210. While Burris poses questions which would be good for interviewing police candidates, I think they would also be most appropriate for soul–searching on this topic.

I implore you not to be insulted by the existence of entities such as internal affairs. If your actions are guided by ethical decisions, these entities can be your saving grace. They are designed to be fact finders in search of the truth. Moreover, those walking with integrity should never fear the existence of any screening mechanism designed to get to know you better. Although I cannot assure you that because you behave ethically throughout your career that everything will be wonderful, I can assure that it should alleviate worry and a host of other problems.

Chapter 21

The A to Z for building a solid foundation for your Criminal Justice Career

A — Anticipate what is expected of you with respect to your background both professionally and personally.

B — Background – Since past behavior is widely believed to be the best predictor for future behavior, understand that your background is your bridge to the future.

C — Character is something you build not that you are born with. You can start to build your character right now.

D — Dependability is a key ingredient of demonstrating integrity.

E — Ethics is everywhere in every decision you make. Embrace them early and endeavor to engage in ethical decision–making.

F — Freedom. There is a freedom in behaving ethically. It eliminates a substantial degree of worry.

G — Goodness. Contrary to what many may say, we know intrinsically what is good, and even what is "goodness." When faced with two choices, endeavor to do good and you will be on the right track.

H — Help yourself and others by showing, illustrating, and thus paving the way for those who appear to be stumbling when it comes to doing the right thing.

I — Integrity is who you are and what you do when no one is looking. Strive to always do what is right and do not be surprised if someone really was looking. Introspectively look inside from time to time to see if you like what is there.

J — "Just Do It" to coin a phrase. Beginning to build character is something you can start at any time. The sooner, the better—especially since one very bad decision depending on the seriousness or the sequence of events it stirs may be enough to eliminate possibilities.

K — Kill any pressure (inside or outside) that will influence you compromising your integrity.

L— Learn, Learn, Learn. Learn from your mistakes; learn from other's mistakes. Study persons you believe are of high moral character as well as those you believe are not. You can learn from each of these two groups; such as values, decisions and behavior to adopt or model as well as those to avoid.

M — Make it happen. Only you can act for you.

N — Nonsense. Avoid it at all cost. Frequently trouble can be avoided if nonsense is avoided.

O — Others can affect your values, integrity and character and consequently how others see you. Choose those you associate with wisely—you will likely affect each other.

P — Pause. Sometimes you need to stop and think before speaking or acting. The extra time you take to think through a situation may make all the difference. P can also represent Past; remember your past can affect your future.

Q — Query – ask questions. Do not assume you know the pitfalls of a given situation without first checking it out in terms of what it means to you or what it can mean to you in the future.

R — Reflect especially on very bad or very good decisions you have already made. It will help you decide ethically in the future.

S — Stop, Look, and listen. Recall the old. Sometimes you need to take extra time and evaluate a situation before making a decision.

T — Timing. It has been stated that "timing is everything." Making ethically motivated decisions is always the right time.

U — Understand yourself and potential weak areas in your values—then go on to strengthen them.

V — Value your values. They may not be like everyone else's but as time goes on, you will see just how valuable your values can be.

W — Will yourself to do the right thing. Your will is 100% in your own hands.

X — "X" yourself from situations and persons who will erode or otherwise adversely affect your values, ethics or integrity.

Y — You can make a difference by doing the right thing. Your ethical behavior will not only benefit you, but others who may be watching you, even if you do not see them.

Z — Which is commonly the end—remember with ethics, there is no finish line. It is the never ending story.

Life Application Exercise

Think about what others will say about your character when you retire.

Chapter 22

Conclusion

As I said in the beginning of this book, it is not written from the perspective of someone who is perfect. Quite the contrary; however, I must admit that since I strive to be one who is credible to provide advice on the topic, I reflect more and more on my own decision–making. With each passing day, this extra scrutiny, I believe is the key to making superior choices closer to right than wrong and so I urge you do so as well. For example, through careful introspection I have found that when faced with two ways of doing something that both seem to be the right thing, if I study them close enough one of them will stand out as superior—and I, as you undoubtedly as well, have not been surprised by the fact that the superior choice usually seems to be more costly and the harder of the two. But trust me, while it may be more difficult to do the righter thing, when you look back (almost immediately) you will know it was for the best; and as an afterthought it will not seem as costly either.

A word to the wise— losing or eroding your integrity may not seem as implausible as you may believe. It starts very gradually and then before you have taken an opportunity to contemplate it—your decisions have changed. How you think has changed. I guard my integrity closely; for fear that the unthinkable happens. Notice, I do not say happen to me because I think if it happens it is because I would have had to have played a role in it. The only hope is to refuse to play such a destructive role.

Let me give you an example of something I witnessed that concerned me. Once I was involved in scoring some documents with others when I noted a disturbing trend. Rather than the information before us being the primary consideration in determining scores, I noticed that the persons most strong– willed or loudest seemed to have significant influence. Having witnessed this tendency in others, I not only resisted myself but also conveyed my concerns to the rest of the group. I challenge you to do likewise. Those who sit and watch things they believe to be wrong without attempting to intervene just promote a code of silence and eventually will move from being a passive partner to an active partner in progressively serious situations.

It is recognized that the standards and examples presented in this book may not be ideals you have ever given much thought to. Moreover, even after learning about them you may feel you do not measure up now—nor that you ever will. These are standards. You can measure up to them if you want to. But you have to change your thinking if you want to change your behavior. I submit that if becoming a criminal justice professional is important to you; you can change your thinking and thus your decision–making and actions. These ethical principles should be part of your life though. If most of this is foreign to you—it may be too hard. I mean this from the standpoint of the reasons people go into public service. People have said they enter public service in the field of criminal justice because they have a strong sense of justice, and fairness. Consequently, they believe they can do the right thing to facilitate principles.

To give you an idea of the type of passion I am speaking of, I will declare this: More than anything occupationally, I wish to be put out of work. For this to happen it would mean that a serious social problem our nation faces would no longer exist—and for that, I would gladly change occupations and do something else. I am not alone. Many who work in the criminal justice system wish that there was no need for their positions which would mean that crime no longer existed. Realistic or not, that is what many of us yearn for.

Final Life Application Exercise

Are you doing the right thing for the right reason? Why do you want to be a criminal justice professional? Where do your motives originate—from within or outside of yourself?

Examine your answers. Assign some weight to your reasons. Are most of your reasons based on what you want to do for others, the agency or yourself? Are most of your reasons related to you personally or do most of them suggest that you are interested in serving the public? Will you work towards the agency's mission? Or are your answers based primarily on what you will receive? 25 years or more is a long time. If most of your rationale for going into public service is based on benefits you expect to receive versus what you plan to give, think about this some more. I recommend a study of public service to understand what may be required. Also do not forget to examine the mission statement of agencies you are considering working for. There is nothing wrong with expecting benefits such as salary, healthcare, job security and other fringes; however, if money or power is your primary reason for going into public service—you will soon want more money and more fringes—all of which is limited—you may likely soon become discontent or worse corrupt.

I wish you well in your quest to find the right job for you—whether it is in the field of criminal justice or something equally rewarding, fulfilling, fascinating and altruistic. May you have the kind of good luck as some have defined as "when preparation meets opportunity."[74] You have taken an important step by preparing yourself to become ethically marketable in reading this book. Now meet opportunity head on!

---

[74] The most recent time I heard this definition of good luck was on November 6, 2003 by Ernest Collins, Marketing Specialist, and Exxon Mobil during his greeting at the convocations and installation of Prairie View A & M University President George Carlton Wright.

References

9th Circuit decision backs medicinal marijuana users. (2003, December 16). Associated Press.

Abuse, Addiction & Recovery (DVDs, Videos, CD–ROMs & Posters). (2003, Fall). Cambridge Educational, p 6.

Agency Backs Lie Detectors Despite Study. (2003, April 21). Federal Employees Digest, 52(7).

Anderson, C. (2003, October). More people find tax cheating acceptable as IRS. Audits plummet 60 percent since 1988. Newsroom@S–T.com.

Barker, T. & Roebuck, J. (1974). An Empirical Typology of Police Corruption. Springfield, IL: Charles C. Thomas. Belluck, P. (2001, April 21). Desperate for Prison Guards, Some States Even Rob Cradles. New York Times.

Bright, J. (2003). "Clean Dirt," A Memoir of Johnnie Mae Gibson, FBI Special Agent. Bloomington, IN.

Bureau of Justice Statistics. (2003). Background Checks for Firearm Transfers, 2002; September, 2003 (NCJ 200116).

Bureau of Justice Statistics. (2003). Survey of State Criminal History Information Systems, 2001; September, 2003 (NCJ 200343).

Bureau of Justice Statistics. (2001). Traffic Stop Data Collection Policies for State Police, 2001; December, 2001 (NCJ 191158).

Burris, J. (1999). Blue vs. Black: Let's End the Conflict Between Cops and Minorities. New York: St. MartinÆs Press.

Butler, D., Gregory. L., & Ray, A. (1995). America's Dumbest Criminals. Nashville, TN: Rutledge Hill Press.

Campanile, C. & Robinson, E. (2001, August 21). Poll ranks NYU top school in 'weed'ing. New York Post.

Carlson, D. (2003). Ethics Roll Call. Plano, TX: Center for Law Enforcement Ethics.

Causey, M. (2003, April 21). Credit Card Abuse. Federal Employee Digest.

Cooper, A. (2003, June 16). Are kids lying more these days? CNN.

Daniel, L. (2003). 2003 Federal Personnel Guide. Washington, D.C.: Key Communications Group, Inc.

Denied Employment After Background Investigation. (2003, November 24). Federal Employees Digest, 53(18).

Department of Justice (website). (2003, June 21 access date). www.usdoj.gov/usao/eousa/foia.

Department of Labor (1988, September). Employee Polygraph Protection Act (Notice; WH Publication 1462).

Delattre, E. (1989). Character and Cops: Ethics in Policing. Washington, D.C.: University Press of America.

Farrell, G. (2004, May 21). Witness in Martha Stewart trial charged with perjury. USA Today.

Feldstein, D. (2003, June 4). Indicted firm's owner donating funds to DA. Houston Chronicle, 21A, 32A.

Feuer, A. (2000, April 16). Drug War Ensnares an Army Colonel Who Fought It. New York Times.

Fitzgerald, J. (2003, July 1). Drug–Law Activist Axed from Laurel Y Bus–Driving Job. Billings Gazette.

Friedman, S. (Executive Producer). (2003, April 18). Today Show. New York: NBC.

Friedman, S. (Executive Producer). (2003, June 2). Today Show. New York: NBC.

Friedman, S. (Executive Producer). (2003, July 17). Today Show. New York: NBC.

Geller, A. (2004, January 15). Gov't To Overhaul Employee Drug Test. Associated Press.

Gilmartin, K. & Harris, J. (1998, January). Law Enforcement Ethics...The Continuum of Compromise. Police Chief Magazine

Ginsberg, S. (2004, January 2). TSA Chief At Dulles Is Charged With DWI. Washington Post, B01.

Harris, R. (1999, April 8). Unabomber's brother, victim urge bridge between families. Associated Press. www.unabombertrial.com/archive.

Hartley, E. (2003, October 31). Lawmakers Target Drugged Drivers. The Annapolis Capital.

Havill, A. (2001). The Spy Who Stayed Out In The Cold: The Secret Life Of FBI Double Agent Robert Hanssen. New York: St. Martin's Press.

Hull, L. (2003, October 9). New plates could deter drunk driving. Times LeaderONLINE and Associated Press. Www.timesleaderonline.com

Investigators Find Widespread IRS Internet Abuse. (2003, June 30). Federal Employees News Digest.

Kellogg, A. (2003, August 29). UMass president resigns amidst political pressure. The Daily Free Press (The Independent Student Newspaper at Boston University).

Kozaryn, L. (2002, April 8). DoD fighting government credit card abuse. Dcmilitary.com.

Koch, E. (2000, December 8). Let's Give Drug Offenders a Second Chance. Newsday.

Lawmakers Seek Regulating Feds' Credit Card Use. (2003, October 27). Federal Employees News Digest.

Le, C. (2003, November 18). Unabomber's brother speaks, Delivers his message against capital punishment. UTICAOD.COM.

Levinson, A. (2001, July 15). No federal aid for college students with drug conviction. Staten Island Sunday Advance.

Malinowski, W. & Stanton, M. (2003, November 19). Affair Ends Agent's Career. Providence Journal.

McCoy, K. (2000, July 16). High Cost of Bad Cops, City shells out $177 million to settle police misconduct cases. Daily News.

McVicker, S. & Khanna, R. (2003, June 4). Indicted firm's owner donating funds to DA. Houston Chronicle, 21A, 32A.

Moose wants chance to talk. (2003, July). American Police Beat, 10 (7) 11.

Morrison, D. (2000, July 28). Some Officers Cash In on Gun Amnesty. USA Today. 17A

New FBI agents say they're going broke. (2003, July). American Police Beat, 10 (7) 17.

New Jersey Troopers Avoid Prosecution in Racial Profiling Case. (2002, January 15). Public Agenda Online.

New Mexico governor calls for legalizing drugs. (1999, October 6). CNN.com

News (Fraud). (2003, May). //A:/News2003//.htm

NIH (2002, August 15). NIH Policy Manual, Official Use of Government Motor Vehicles. www1.od.nih.gov.

OYEZ, U.S. Supreme Court Multimedia, www.oyez.org/oyez/resource. (1/8/04).

Patterson, J. & Kim, P. (1991). The Day America Told the Truth: What People Really Believe About Everything that Really Matters. New York: Prentice Hall Press.

Pentagon Moves to Stop Credit Card Abuse. (2002, March 28). The New York Times.

Reaves, B. & Hickman, M. (2002, October). Census of State and Local Law Enforcement Agencies, 2000. Bureau of Justice Statistics. NCJ 194. NCJ 194066.

Report Details FBI Dismissals, Bad Behavior. (2004, March 1). Federal Employees News Digest.

Ross, S. (Executive Producer). (2003, July 19). Good Morning America. New York: American Broadcasting Service.

Safe in School, Brooklyn Teacher is Booked on Heroin Rap, NY Post, 11/19/99).

Schneider, G. (2003, January 3). Arrested TSA Chief is Ex–Secret Service Agent. Washington Post, A11.

Secret Service Employee Takes Advantage of 9/11. (2004, April 19). Federal Employees News Digest.

Singer, B. (Producer). (2003, July 12). Access Hollywood. Court TV.

Stapley, G. (2004, January 10). Peterson survey data in doubt. Sacramento Bee.

Supreme Court Backs Employer in Refusal to Rehire Ex–Addict. (2003, December 23). Drug Enforcement Report: The Washington Letter on Narcotics, Dangerous Drug, and Marijuana Control.

Supreme Court of the United States, Syllabus, Maryland v. Pringle, No. 02–809, by Reporter of Decisions.

Troopers resign over videotape. (2003, July). American Police Beat, 10(7) 7.

United States Department of Justice, Office of Justice Programs, Office for Victims of Crime (1998). New Directions from the Field: Victims' Rights and Services for the 21st Century, Law Enforcement.

Zakheim, D., (2002, June 27). Department of Defense (memo).

Order Form

Your shipping address:

Name		
Agency		
Address		
City	State	Zip
Daytime telephone (with area code)	Internet E–Mail address (optional)	

Your order:

Please send me the following order:		QTY	Totals
Becoming Ethically Marketable	**$29.95 each**		$
Sales Tax	Add 7.75% Sales Tax for items shipped to California addresses		$
Shipping	$3.00 for the first book and $1.50 for each additional book		$
TOTAL	Enclose check, money order, or purchase order payable in US funds to "Staggs Publishing"		$

Government Purchase Orders and Personal Checks are Accepted!
You may order ON–LINE at http://www.staggspublishing.com/orders.html

CREDIT CARD ORDERS	AMEX VISA MasterCard DISCOVER
Card Number:	Expiration Date (Mo/Yr):
Cardholder Name:	Card type: ☐ VISA ☐ MasterCard
Authorized Signature:	☐ American Express ☐ Discover

Thank you! Please mail your orders to:

Staggs Publishing
P.O. Box 1565
Wildomar, CA 92595–1565

Credit Card Orders and Purchase Orders may be faxed to (909)244–0098

Questions? Call (909)244–0098 or E–Mail orders@staggspublishing.com

These books have unconditional guarantees. If you are not satisfied with any book you may return it for a full refund at anytime. Quantity discounts are available for agencies and educators on orders of 11 or more books. Write or contact the publisher at (909)244–2278 for further information.